"*Think God's a joke?* Join former skeptic Guillaume Bignon on his journey so you can consider what he found. *Having doubts about your faith?* Let the answers Guillaume discovered bolster your beliefs. *Want to help family and friends find faith?* Give them a copy of *Confessions of a French Atheist* and let God use this compelling story to open their hearts and minds. There is something good for everyone in this powerful new book!"

MARK MITTELBERG, executive director of the Lee Strobel Center for Evangelism and Applied Apologetics at Colorado Christian University; author of *The Questions Christians Hope No One Will Ask (With Answers)* and *Contagious Faith: Discover Your Natural Style for Sharing Jesus with Others*

"In *Confessions of a French Atheist*, Guillaume Bignon tells of his conversion story, and it is not only honest but also winsomely vulnerable. Bignon's book brings together the moral and rational, the existential and the philosophical, and it reveals how the gospel of Christ satisfies our deepest human longings while also addressing humanity's most fundamental intellectual questions. Read this book and pass it on to others!"

PAUL COPAN, Pledger Family Chair of Philosophy and Ethics, Palm Beach Atlantic University; author of *Loving Wisdom: A Guide to Philosophy and Christian Faith*

"Philosopher Guillaume Bignon's search for meaning took him from Paris to New York, from womanizing to marriage, and from a hedonistic brand of atheism to a thoughtful faith in Jesus. *Confessions of a French Atheist* is a gripping spiritual memoir and intellectual 'apology' that will engage the reader's heart and mind."

PETER S. WILLIAMS, assistant professor in communication and worldviews at Gimlekollen NLA University College, Kristiansand, Norway; author of *Outgrowing God? A Beginner's Guide to Richard Dawkins and the God Debate*

"Guillaume Bignon's story is simply incredible, just another example of a thoroughly committed atheist determined to discredit Jesus and Christianity who then gets turned upside down when forced to face the facts—the facts of Jesus' life and the facts of his own life."

GREGORY KOUKL, president of Stand to Reason; author of *Tactics: A Game Plan for Discussing Your Christian Convictions* and *The Story of Reality: How the World Began, How It Ends, and Everything Important that Happens in Between*

"A delightful and enchanting read—just try to put it down! This fast-paced and well-written volume recounts a search for meaning in a seemingly meaningless world, interspersed with philosophical tidbits. What happens when atheistic intellectualism meets sophisticated apologetic arguments? Read on . . ."

GARY R. HABERMAS, distinguished research professor at Liberty University

"*Confessions* is a captivating story of romance, betrayal, redemption, and a winsome presentation of a rational Christian faith. Guillaume's journey, like so many, tells us of how wretched we are and yet how powerful God's grace is. An inspiring book for all people."

KURT JAROS, theologian at Veracity Hill; executive director of Defenders Media; affiliate faculty at Colorado Christian University

"As a brilliant, talented, and successful man, former atheist Guillaume Bignon had no need for God. In this transparent autobiography, he takes us along his unexpected journey into the question of belief and a closer exploration into his own life. Through earnest searching, honest wrestling, and reflection, he confronts his own false presumptions about atheism, Christianity, and even himself, and he finds life-changing truth in surprising ways."

JANA HARMON, teaching fellow for the C. S. Lewis Institute; host of the *Side B Podcast*

"Guillaume has written an incredibly readable and searingly honest account of his journey from atheism to Christian faith, masterfully weaving together the intellectual, emotional, and spiritual aspects of his journey. Apologetics can often be a 'dry' subject. This book is the opposite. Yes, *Confessions of a French Atheist* is packed with rational arguments for the truth of Christianity, but it is also a no-holds-barred account of how God graciously shows up in the messiness of our personal lives. Read it and then give it to the next intellectual enquirer you meet."

JUSTIN BRIERLEY, host of the *Unbelievable?* radio show and podcast; author of *Unbelievable?: Why, After Ten Years of Talking with Atheists, I'm Still Christian*

"My thoughts on *Confessions of a French Atheist* can be captured in one word: *fantastic*. It is captivating and insightful. I couldn't put it down. It gets my highest recommendation for believers, seekers, and skeptics."

SEAN MCDOWELL, apologetics professor at Biola University; coauthor of *Evidence that Demands a Verdict*

"I have long thought—from both my readings and friendships— that the French *do* atheism better than pretty much anyone else. But Guillaume Bignon's *Confessions of a French Atheist* shows that the French can also make the best public advocates for the Christian faith. Here is a story full of culture, verve, thoughtfulness, emotion, and intelligence. Bignon is as comfortable discussing romance, sex, and beauty as he is science, history, and philosophy. The arguments here are strong and so are the aesthetics. If France has long represented the leading edge of a post-Christian society, a book like this shows there is a way back, not to Christendom but to Christ himself."

JOHN DICKSON, historian, author, and host of *Undeceptions*; lecturer and research associate at University of Sydney; distinguished fellow at Ridley College

"A superb and engaging lesson in philosophy, theology, and crystal-clear Christian apologetics, all propelled by an honest and captivating personal narrative. What a perfect book to get into the hands of skeptics and also into the hands of believers who find themselves struggling with doubt. Guillaume Bignon strikes just the right balance of head and heart to make this a true faith-building experience for anyone who is blessed to read it."

CRAIG J. HAZEN, founder and director of the graduate program in Christian apologetics at Biola University; author of *Five Sacred Crossings* and *Fearless Prayer*

"Guillaume Bignon weaves his own fascinating story with clear, persuasive explanations of the evidence that led him as a self-indulgent atheist to devote his life to serving the God who has revealed himself in Jesus Christ. Readers unfamiliar with the intellectual tradition of French unbelief are in for a treat as Bignon introduces such skeptical luminaries as Voltaire, Baron d'Holbach, Ernest Renan, and Prosper Alfaric and cogently engages their objections to Christianity. Colorful illustrations drawn from everything from volleyball to Disney movies make his answers fun and memorable. Yet it is the story of Bignon's personal conversion, with the surprising twists and the highs, lows, and messiness of real life, that make it hard to put this book down."

ROBERT M. BOWMAN JR., author of *Faith Thinkers: 30 Christian Apologists You Should Know*

"In *Confessions of a French Atheist*, Guillaume Bignon recounts his journey from a hedonistic lifestyle, in which he was scornful of those who believed in God, to experiencing the grace and forgiveness of Christ. Bignon tells of how he sought to fill the void of spiritual emptiness in his life with sexual indulgence, seducing women and using them for his own gratification, sometimes at the expense of other friendships. Eventually, a relationship with a Christian woman led him to investigate the truth claims of the Bible and ultimately become a Christian. Bignon's writing style is extremely engaging, and the book is a gripping page-turner. In addition to recounting Bignon's journey from atheism to Christianity, the book offers a concise introduction to some of the key lines of evidence for the existence of God and the veracity of the gospel. The book also contains a compelling exposé of what the message of the gospel is and why we should care. I will definitely be recommending this book to friends interested in learning more about Jesus and how he can transform a person's life."

JONATHAN MCLATCHIE, assistant professor of biology at Sattler College; fellow of the Discovery Institute

"In *Confessions of a French Atheist*, Guillaume Bignon says that he went into a church 'like someone would go to the zoo: to see exotic animals he had heard of but never actually seen.' In this book, you'll read about an exotic creature you've neither heard about nor seen: a ridiculously intelligent and witty French athlete questioning his way into the Kingdom of God."

DAVID WOOD, Acts 17 Apologetics

"More than sixteen centuries ago, Augustine told us why he had rehearsed his licentious past in the pages of his *Confessions*: 'The recalling of my wicked ways is bitter in my memory, but I do it so that you may be sweet to me.' Like Augustine's *Confessions*, Guillaume Bignon's *Confessions of a French Atheist* tells a story of loss—lost relationships, ambitions, and dreams—largely owed to a seared conscience and a skewed worldview. But it also tells a story of renewal—fresh faith, meaning, and purpose—brought about by a quickened conscience and a quest for truth. For both Augustine and Bignon, hindsight of God's guiding hand through it all shows he is sweet. I can give these pages no higher praise than saying they caused me to revel in God's sovereignty and relish his sweetness. I pray they will do the same for every person who providentially partakes of them."

J. ED KOMOSZEWSKI, coauthor of *Reinventing Jesus and Putting Jesus in His Place*

"In *Confessions of a French Atheist*, the author weaves a chaotic piece of fabric, with frayed threads in a seemingly purposeless design. He is unafraid to reveal the twisted, ugly backside of his own story—both before and after his conversion. But the reader gradually, step by step, sees the cloth from the other side, a beautiful tapestry woven by the Master himself. Bignon's narrative is the embodiment of Romans 8:28, a very personal testimony that there are no coincidences in the story of redemption."

DANIEL B. WALLACE, senior research professor of New Testament Studies, Dallas Theological Seminary

• • •

Confessions of a French Atheist

How God Hijacked My Quest
to Disprove the Christian Faith

Confessions
of a French
Atheist

Guillaume Bignon

FOREWORD BY LEE STROBEL

TYNDALE
MOMENTUM®

A Tyndale nonfiction imprint

Visit Tyndale online at tyndale.com.

Visit Tyndale Momentum online at tyndalemomentum.com.

Tyndale, Tyndale's quill logo, *Tyndale Momentum,* and the Tyndale Momentum logo are registered trademarks of Tyndale House Ministries. Tyndale Momentum is a nonfiction imprint of Tyndale House Publishers, Carol Stream, Illinois.

Designed by Eva M. Winters

Published in association with the literary agency of Mark Sweeney & Associates, Carol Stream, Illinois.

An earlier version of this book was published in French as *La foi a ses raisons: Confessions d'un athée surpris par Dieu* [Faith has its reasons: Confessions of an atheist surprised by God].

Some names have been changed for the privacy of individuals.

For information about special discounts for bulk purchases, please contact Tyndale House Publishers at csresponse@tyndale.com, or call 1-800-323-9400.

Library of Congress Cataloging-in-Publication Data
A catalog record for this book is available from the Library of Congress.

ISBN 978-1-4964-4302-1

Printed in the United States of America

28 27 26 25 24 23 22
7   6   5   4   3   2   1

Contents

• • •

Foreword

• • •

AS AN AUTHOR, I LOVE STORIES. As a journalist, I especially appreciate *true* stories—unflinchingly honest accounts that trace a person's circuitous route as they seek to resolve personal challenges. That's what Guillaume Bignon provides in this compelling spiritual memoir, tracing his fascinating quest for answers to life's most profound questions while deftly weaving in arguments and evidence for Christianity that helped him along the way.

Actually, I see much of myself in Guillaume's book. Both of us started as atheists who endured forced church attendance when we were younger. We were each prompted to investigate the claims of Christianity because of a relationship with a woman who was a believer. I employed my training in journalism and law; Guillaume drew upon the highly disciplined mind that led him into a successful career as a software engineer.

Both of us critically examined historical data, scientific findings, and philosophical reasoning. In the end, we reached our verdicts—but don't let me spoil the climax of Guillaume's story. There's much that differs from my own life experience.

Through it all, Guillaume candidly describes his life as an accomplished athlete with a Frenchman's eye for romance. He doesn't shy away from admitting his mistakes and short-comings. Clearly, he's conversant with historic and contemporary atheistic writings; indeed, he gives due consideration to their claims.

What I like the most, though, is the way he evaluates the evidence in much the same way that a referee judges one of his championship volleyball matches. Setting aside prejudices and preconceived notions, he lets the case for Christianity unfold regardless of his own preferences. In other words, he allows the facts to speak for themselves and the arguments to point him toward conclusions he had not anticipated—and which, in some cases, ran contrary to his preferences.

As a baseball fan, I liken it to allowing the umpire to call a ball a ball and a strike a strike. Let the scoreboard tally the results. This, in short, can be a model for other spiritual seekers as they embark on their own pursuit for answers.

Along the way, Guillaume finds resolution to some of the vexing questions that had haunted him as a young man who had achieved much. What is success? What defines happiness? Where do we find a reliable framework for morality? All of us wrestle with these issues at some point—and I believe you will resonate with how Guillaume chases the answers.

So turn the page and read on. Let Guillaume's personal story draw you in as he jets from Paris to an exotic Caribbean island to New York City. Then allow his insightful evaluation of philosophy, history, and science to challenge your notions of reality. Call a ball a ball and a strike a strike—and see how your conclusions might change your life and even your eternity.

I'll tell you what: You'd be hard pressed to find a more amiable and engaging companion on your journey than my friend Guillaume Bignon.

Lee Strobel
Author of *The Case for Christ* and *The Case for Heaven*

1

Hooked in the Caribbean

• • •

Destiny is written concurrently with
the event, not prior to it.

JACQUES MONOD

I DIDN'T EXPECT A VACATION in the Caribbean to change my life forever. Somehow, it did.

Around the time I graduated from college, my uncle Jean-Jacques took a job that required a move to the island of Saint Martin, about twelve hundred miles southeast of Miami. I had never heard of the place and had no idea how breathtakingly beautiful it was.

Shortly after their move, my aunt and uncle sent us some photos of their new life in paradise—various shots of my cousins with big smiles on their faces, sitting on the trunk of a twisted palm tree or reclining on a beach whose colors were so pure and dazzling it seemed they had to have been

Photoshopped. The sand was perfectly white, the water a hypnotizing turquoise blue, and the sun so bright that the colors fairly jumped off the page.

They seem to be enjoying their new life, I thought, but the idea of crossing the Atlantic from Paris to visit them never entered my mind, even when my parents bought themselves tickets for a short vacation there. But when they returned home, looking tanned and healthy, they began touting the island with a missionary zeal.

"Nicolas, Guillaume, Estelle," they said to my siblings and me, "at least once in your life, you've got to see it! In fact, whenever you want to go—all three of you—we'll buy you each a ticket to Saint Martin. And you should go as soon as possible."

What an offer!

Nicolas was the first to take them up on it. I would have gone with him, but I had just started a job as a software engineering consultant in the finance industry and hadn't yet accrued enough vacation time. Nicolas soon returned, suntanned, relaxed, and just as excited about the island as our parents had been. So much so that when I took my vacation in Saint Martin the following July, he decided to go back with me.

Paradise found

Aunt Irene picked us up at Princess Juliana International Airport, in the Dutch territory on the south end of the tropical island. As soon as I stepped off the airplane, I was enveloped in a thick blanket of heat and humidity—just as everyone had warned. I quickly decided that I'd rather be at the beach than in a hot car, and that's immediately where we went. In fact, we had scarcely pulled out of the parking lot before my aunt stopped the car at Maho Beach, a tiny stretch of pure white sand just off the end of the airport runway. You really need to see it to believe it. The only thing separating the beach from the landing strip is a narrow road and a chain-link fence. Pilots on approach fly very low over Maho Beach so they can touch down just a few dozen meters beyond. Enormous airplanes zoom so close over the sunbathers that I felt I could bounce a soccer ball off one of them if I gave it a good kick. I had never seen anything like it. My exotic vacation was off to an amazing start.

No sooner had my aunt stopped the car than Nicolas leapt out, ripped off his shorts and T-shirt, and immediately dove into the water as if his life depended on it. All I could do was laugh. He had endured an eight-hour flight with his bathing suit on under his clothes just so he could pull that stunt for me. But when I entered the water a few minutes later, I understood his urgency. The waters of the Caribbean were just as beautiful as the photos suggested and so warm that I didn't feel even a hint of a chill upon entering. Saint Martin seriously ruined every other beach for me.

We spent our time on the island sunbathing, sipping cocktails, swimming, and even playing a little bit of beach volleyball. There was a court set up next to the most beautiful beach on Orient Bay. My uncle's house was located just behind this heavenly spot. While we were there, I often woke up early to run on the beach in preparation for my first season playing in the nationals in volleyball, which would start in September. It took us only about two minutes to get to Orient Bay by foot, but we often took my aunt's car so we could visit the rest of the island and see other beaches as well. Life was good.

With all these exotic distractions, I had almost forgotten about running after girls. This was somewhat surprising, given the focus of my life over the past several years. But because Nicolas and I didn't really go out in the evening—at least not to clubs or bars—we didn't often find ourselves in places where we would meet eligible young ladies.

Until one day they came to *us*.

Hitchhiking and the American girls

Nicolas and I had spent a day at the beach with our younger cousin, Alexandre. We were on the Dutch end of the island, pretty far from Orient Bay. I don't remember how we got down there, but I know we didn't have a car and would have to improvise on how to get back. When it was time to pack up and leave, I figured our only choice was to walk home, maybe an hour's trek on foot. But Nicolas had another idea: "Why don't we hitchhike?"

I had never hitchhiked before and wasn't sure how I felt about it. It seemed strange to stick out your thumb and expect someone to give you a ride. But Nicolas was undeterred. With a big smile on his face, he put his thumb in the air, and less than two minutes later, a little purple car stopped on the side of the road. When we walked over, we saw two young ladies inside. The slightly embarrassed driver rolled down her window and spoke to us in English with an American accent.

"Can you please help us?"

They hadn't stopped to pick us up; they needed directions!

"We just arrived this afternoon, and now we're lost somewhere between the airport and our hotel."

Just our luck. But we were well-mannered young men who were certainly willing to assist two young ladies. (Especially two *attractive* young ladies.)

"Where are you going?" my brother asked.

"Esmeralda Resort."

Magnifique! Esmeralda Resort is right on Orient Bay, which made us all neighbors.

Nicolas grinned and said, "Take us with you, and we'll show you right where it is."

The driver looked a little hesitant, but her passenger seemed pretty excited about picking up three good-looking Frenchmen in swimsuits. She finally convinced her friend, and Nicolas, Alexandre, and I squeezed into the back seat of their little rental car.

The driver's name was Vanessa, and she was from New York. Her friend, Tasha, was from Miami. They were both gorgeous. Tasha was a platinum blonde with big blue eyes and the features of a model. Vanessa had long, perfectly curled brown hair, blue-green eyes, and a captivating smile. Though she now had a job in finance, she had formerly worked as an actress and model.

I felt we had hit the jackpot! On the way to the hotel, Nicolas and I made good use of our French accents to flirt with the two ladies. I knew we had to try to see them again. Our Gallic charm must have worked because, when we arrived at the Esmeralda Resort, they gave us their room number and agreed to get together with us later that day.

In the meantime, Nicolas and I had two things to discuss: which girl did we each prefer, and where could we take them on the island to show them a good time?

The answer to the first question was easy enough: I liked the girl with the curly hair and Nicolas was interested in the blonde. As for where we would go, Nicolas told me to leave it up to him. This was not his first trip to the island, and he had a plan.

When we stopped by later that day, Vanessa answered the door. Tasha was just awakening from a nap, so we stayed outside to give her time to gather herself. Vanessa stepped out onto the patio with us, and we chatted for a few minutes while waiting for her friend.

Inevitably, the question of what we did for a living came up, and I managed to wrap my reply in a thin veil of false modesty as I explained that I worked as a software engineer, played keyboards in a rock band, and was also a championship volleyball player—all true, but also couched in a way meant to impress this young woman and make sure she'd want to see me again. But when Tasha finally joined us, it was Nicolas who played our best card.

"How would you like to go to Pinel Island?"

Pinel Island is an uninhabited islet at the north end of Orient Bay. Accessible only by boat, it has beautiful beaches, trails for hiking, reefs for snorkeling, and two beachfront restaurants. What more could you ask for?

"Pinel is even better than Saint Martin," Nicolas assured everyone. "You'll be blown away!"

After some discussion of the island's merits, we agreed to meet the next morning for a day trip.

Budding romance and a bombshell

Tasha and Vanessa arrived at the boat landing in beachwear, and we prepared to embark. While we were getting into the boat, Nicolas and I both noticed something we hadn't seen before: Tasha had a ring on her left hand. Too bad for Nicolas. I had already called dibs on Vanessa, and what's more, I was starting to think she was interested in me, as well.

When we arrived on Pinel, we naturally paired off into couples, and Vanessa and I soon found ourselves swimming alone together in the lagoon. After talking for a while and gazing into each other's eyes, we began to kiss, and I was over the moon.

Nicolas and Tasha eventually reappeared, and we found a table—just lounging chairs, really—at one of the two restaurants on the island. The waiter, a young French guy inspired by the presence of the two American women, kept stopping by in his bathing suit to serve us unlimited artisanal, infused rum cocktails. Soaking in the beauty of my companion and the heavenly setting, I soon was intoxicated—both figuratively and literally. By the end of the afternoon, with the combination of sun and alcohol, I was feeling pretty woozy.

What a waste, I thought. I had used all my powers of seduction, only to have the day ruined by cocktails I didn't even enjoy.

If I get sick in front of everyone, this relationship is over. Please, please, please don't let that happen!

I wasn't praying to anyone in particular, but my prayer was answered. Though the trip back to Saint Martin was rough on my stomach, I didn't lose my lunch. My budding romance with Vanessa still had a chance.

The rest of the week that the women were on Saint Martin, the four of us got together several times, mostly on the beach at Orient Bay. I remember being flabbergasted when Vanessa told me that she and Tasha were staying for only ten days because that was all the vacation time they had. In France, the legal minimum for paid vacation is five weeks, and the average is more like seven. I met Vanessa midway through my three-and-a-half weeks on the island, and I was quite annoyed at how little time she and I would have together before she had to leave.

One afternoon, while Vanessa and I were lounging on beach chairs and drinking piña coladas, she dropped a bombshell on me. I don't remember exactly how it came up in conversation, but she told me she believed in God.

What!... Seriously?... In the twenty-first century? To me, this was the equivalent of intellectual suicide. I had been raised going to Catholic Mass on Sundays, but I had long since put behind me any thoughts of faith, choosing instead to seek knowledge of the world through valid and rational pursuits such as math and physics. From my perspective, people who believed in God were either steeped in tradition or simply refused to think logically.

"Why?" I asked Vanessa.

"With everything I've seen," she replied, "I can't help but believe."

Her response seemed kind of elusive, but it was clear that there was more to the story. I wasn't inclined to probe any deeper at the time, so I made a mental note to bring it up again later. Surely she could be persuaded to change her thinking if I challenged her beliefs with a minimal dose of reason and common sense.

The second—and more devastating—piece of news she shared was that she believed in abstinence from sex before marriage. This was not at all what I believed—and certainly not what I wanted. I had a history of conquests and intimate relationships, and though I wouldn't say it was the *only* thing I was thinking about with Vanessa, it was certainly *part* of what I had in mind.

At the same time, I knew that Nicolas wasn't having any greater success with Tasha. I don't know exactly what went on between the two of them, but I know they didn't sleep together. I also know I would not have been happy if I were Tasha's husband. That being said, she clearly wasn't available, and their relationship didn't go very far. I, on the other hand, was moving toward a serious relationship with Vanessa, and it looked as if we might have a future even after we left Saint Martin.

Normally, for me at the time, Vanessa's beliefs about sex and God would have been enough to make me turn and run. But I think the combination of her beauty; the romantic notion of falling in love with a foreigner; the fact that she was from New York, which seemed exotic to me in the same way that many Americans think of Paris; and the serendipitous way in which we had met on this paradise island—it all felt like a Hollywood movie in so many ways. So I didn't break up with her when she left for home. I just told myself that the obstacles would take care of themselves in time.

When my vacation ended in Saint Martin, I returned to Paris, and Vanessa and I began a long-distance relationship—which proved to be a bit more complicated than our island romance.

But let's not get ahead of the story.

2

A "Most Tender" Childhood

• • •

*How is it that a Christian can thank God for endowing
us with this fabulous tool of intellect and the power of
logical thought, and then turn around and say that we
must abandon its usage as we strive to know him?*

ALBERT JACQUARD

I WAS RAISED IN THE TOWN of Montigny-le-Bretonneux, south-
west of Versailles but still close enough to Paris by train that
we could easily go into the city. And during my years at
university, I was able to live at home and stay out of debt.

When we were growing up, my brother and sister and
I often went skiing in the winter and spent our summers
at the beach—either on the Mediterranean or the south
Atlantic coast—or at our paternal grandparents' summer
home in Provence. Some of my favorite childhood memories are from their renovated farmhouse between Manosque
and Forcalquier, partly because my summer vacations were
almost entirely devoted to playing—and my grandparents

had a swimming pool—and partly because of the amazing food we ate there. I especially remember the calissons (a traditional French confection made of candied fruit and ground almonds topped with a layer of icing), tapenade from nearby olive groves, and Provençal breakfasts of toasted French sourdough bread covered in butter and local lavender honey. Had I believed in heaven, I imagine it would have looked a lot like Provence.

During my younger days, like any little boy who loves to play, I had countless action figures, Legos, board games, and collectible card games filling my closet, my mind, and my heart. To be truthful, my passion for games bordered on an addiction. I was always the one who suggested playing a game with Nicolas, Estelle, or my parents, Maman and Papa; and when all four agreed to play a board game with me, I felt as if I'd hit the jackpot.

Childish board games soon gave way to fantasy tabletop war games with sculpted miniature models that my brother, sister, and I spent countless hours customizing with special paints and brushes. Some of the figurines turned out really nice, and we discovered a whole new universe of games in which fantastic battles were fought between armies of miniature warriors.

But the *pièce de résistance* came when my parents finally broke down and bought us a Nintendo video console. It surpassed all our expectations. Papa was a computer scientist with a company that manufactured aeronautic equipment, and he had always had computers at home. Though we'd had the privilege of seeing some of the first interactive video games ever made, Nicolas and I had been trying for some time to convince our parents that we needed a gaming system of our own. For a game addict like me, the Nintendo was an overdose of fun.

Though my childhood was "most tender," as we say in France, it was not without its challenges. There were certain obstacles that came between me and my games. One of those was Sunday Mass. Like many French families at the time, mine was nominally Catholic, and we attended Mass nearly every Sunday. Mass is not a particularly exciting event for any little boy, much less when it interferes with playing video games or watching Sunday morning cartoons.

Going to church

My first memories of attending Mass are pretty fuzzy, but I remember well the Church of Saint Martin in the center of Montigny-le-Bretonneux. It was an old stone building, built in the thirteenth century and renovated in 1610. (Yes, I looked it up on the internet.) Today, I find this type of heritage fascinating because I live in the United States where it would be impossible to find a building that old; but at the time, it didn't interest me in the least. The only thing I remember was that the priest, Father Silvano, had a strong Italian accent. I recall how every week, when he celebrated the Eucharist, he said that "Jesus he take-a the bread, he break-a it, and he give it to his disciples, a-saying, take-a and eat-a it." His adding of an extra syllable to most of his verbs made me think he was making a mistake every time he spoke. I remember being amazed that he could repeat the same liturgy week after week and never get it right!

For the priest, as well as the congregation, there are many parts of the liturgy to be memorized and recited during Mass. I didn't find rote memorization very interesting, so the only thing I ever learned was the Lord's Prayer. I recall sitting in my bed with a book where the prayer was printed in big letters, my mom reading it over and over with me until I memorized it. It's the only thing I can remember ever learning that had to do with religion, but I don't recall ever praying it as if God were actually listening. Maman didn't try to make me memorize the Hail Mary prayer, and I never did learn it, despite hearing it every Sunday during Mass.

I also attended catechism class from time to time, but I don't remember much about it. Outside of church or catechism, we never spoke much about God. Even saying grace before meals wasn't part of our routine. After all, it was Maman who had prepared the food!

Simply put, faith in God had no real impact on my life. I can't speak for every member of my family or my close friends; they may very well have had a deeper religious experience than I did. But on the outside, their lives looked just like mine. There was nothing that would have prompted me to ask any deeper questions about God. He simply wasn't a factor.

When I was baptized, just before my first birthday, my parents had asked my uncle Jacques and one of my grandmother's young cousins to be my godparents. But here's the thing: Neither one was a practicing Catholic. Uncle Jacques may have believed in God, but if he did, I never knew about it, and we rarely saw each other anyway. My godmother, on the other hand, was more than just "not really a believer." She was actively opposed to faith in God. In recent years, the few discussions I've had with her about God's existence have led me to understand that she isn't open to discussing the matter; in fact, she finds my faith appalling. Still, she is someone I love very much, and she took excellent care of me when I was a child. She was the most amazing atheist godmother!

Like many kids, I fought my battles with boredom in the pews on Sunday mornings. The one part of the Mass that really bothered me was the Eucharist—because I was excluded. When the time came, everyone stood up, pew by pew, and went forward to receive the sacrament from the priest. But because I hadn't yet made my first Holy Communion, I had to remain seated. So I was understandably quite excited when my turn came for the next step of Catholic initiation.

I don't remember the details of my first Holy Communion; I only have a vague memory of sitting in the sacristy with the other candidates while our catechism teacher taught us how to place our hands to receive the consecrated wafer. I also remember that my parents organized a party in my honor—complete with presents—to celebrate the big event afterward.

Over time, my family changed churches a couple of times, but I don't know why. We still lived in Montigny.

Eventually, we began attending Mass in Saint-Lambert-des-Bois, where Father Doiteau, an old family friend of my father's, was the priest. The church building was ancient, and I remember being fascinated by the old pipe organ. Sometimes we attended Mass on Saturday evening instead of Sunday morning, which held two distinct advantages as far as I was concerned: The Saturday evening liturgy wasn't quite as long, and going to church on Saturday freed us up to watch Sunday morning cartoons.

My few memories about the church in Saint-Lambert include watching the priest walk up and down the aisles with a thurible on the end of a chain. As he swung the shiny metal container, smoky incense filled the sanctuary. I didn't know why he did it, and I didn't ask, but I found it entertaining. I also remember celebrating Palm Sunday, because the church gave everyone palm branches that had been blessed by the priest. We took them home and stuck them behind the crucifixes on our bedroom walls. Once again, I didn't understand the significance of the ritual, but I liked the way the branch looked on my wall.

The way my family celebrated Easter had nothing to do with Jesus. France doesn't have an Easter bunny, but we do have the Cloches de Pâques—flying church bells that drop chocolate eggs and candy into children's backyards. When my parents announced that the bells had visited during the night, my siblings and I would search the yard for treats hidden under the bushes. Every once in a while, we would find a toy—which I preferred to any amount of chocolate. But that was pretty rare. In any event, the resurrection of Jesus was absent from our Easter celebration.

Profession of faith, confirmation, and invalidation

As my second year of middle school approached, so did the next step in my Catholic upbringing: the profession of faith. Also called solemn Communion, this very French ritual involves adolescent Catholics professing their belief in God and publicly affirming that they are taking their parents' faith as their own.

Though I understood that the Church considered this ritual an important step, I wasn't motivated by the theology of it. I was, however, well aware that there would be a party afterward—with presents, of course. On top of that, the preparation for solemn Communion included a three-day retreat with the other candidates, and my mom was in charge of organizing it. So I was in.

I remember being more interested in the girls at the retreat than in the faith I was supposed to be professing, but I do recall asking myself during one of our free periods, *What if I were to read a little bit of the Bible, just to see what's in it?*

When I opened the Bible at random, it fell on the story of Satan tempting Jesus in the desert.[1] Jesus answered the devil three times using the Old Testament (though I had no idea of that at the time), and I was impressed by his talent for repartee. I remember thinking, *Hmm, Jesus had some pretty good comebacks*, but the thought didn't linger for long. To an unbelieving seventh grader, it was just a story, and when the day arrived for my solemn Communion, the faith I "professed" really wasn't my own.

Like the other kids, I wore a white robe for the celebration, with a wooden cross around my neck and a white candle in my hand. Add to that my braces, oversized glasses, and wild, fuzzy hair, and you'll understand why the pictures Maman kept from that event can still be used for blackmail all these years later.

The pictures taken two years later at my confirmation were a bit less disastrous. Once again, I didn't understand much about the theology of the ritual—that I would allegedly receive the Holy Spirit through the laying on of hands, equipping me to live the Christian life and share my faith with others—but I was certain there would be another party in my honor.

I can still remember Nicolas telling me very sincerely before his own confirmation, "Guillaume, you know, we don't do this just for the presents." But a few years later, he more honestly admitted that the gifts (and I don't mean spiritual gifts) were also the motivating factor behind his decision to be confirmed.

The event went off without incident, but I retracted my profession of faith soon after when I told my parents, "I don't believe."

When Nicolas and I reached high school age, Maman and

Papa allowed us more and more freedom, which included choosing whether we wanted to go to Mass. We took full advantage of the opportunity to start sleeping in on Sundays. As was typical, Nicolas led the way in this regard, but when I realized that our parents were okay with his decision, I quickly followed suit. I finally put words to my true confession, admitting verbally what had always been true on the inside: *I was an atheist.*

Adopting a secular point of view

As I began to embrace atheism as a young man, I went far beyond and accepted the presupposition that one had to be stupid to believe in God. This notion has been quite popular in French culture since the eighteenth century. For example, Baron Paul-Henri Thiry d'Holbach, a prolific French philosopher during the Enlightenment, once wrote, "To be a good Christian, it is essential not to have a brain, or at least to have one that's well and truly shrunk."[2] Further, "All good Christians must be in a state of sweet simplicity, predisposing them to believe things that are not in the least bit credible without a second thought, on command of their spiritual guides."[3]

D'Holbach also suggested that "faith is the effect of a grace which God hardly grants to enlightened persons, who are accustomed to consult common sense. It is made only for the minds of men who are incapable of reflection, drunk on enthusiasm, or invincibly attached to the prejudices of childhood."[4]

Today, we find these same presuppositions in the writings

of atheist philosopher Michel Onfray. At the beginning of his *Atheist Manifesto*, Onfray cannot quite bring himself to make a positive statement, even as he tries to sound fair-minded: "I do not despise believers. I find them neither ridiculous nor pathetic."[5] However, as Onfray warms to his polemic, he calls believers in general "naive and foolish" and accuses them of being filled with "neuroses, psychoses, and . . . aberrations," and "a personal mental pathology . . . ushering in a wholesale mental pandemic."[6]

"Atheism," he says, "is not therapy but restored mental health."[7] Believers possess "the minds of children," suffer from "obsessional neurosis" and "hallucinatory psychosis."[8] God "puts to death . . . reason, intelligence and the critical mind."[9] In short, the church is a place where "intelligence is ailing."[10]

I have to wonder what he would say about someone he *does* find ridiculous or pathetic!

To this day, French culture maintains that most Christians must be somewhat simpleminded. For those not so easily dismissed, we must assume there is some reason that an otherwise intelligent individual would believe in something as irrational as God's existence. What possible explanation could there be? I can think of two: Either they adhere to religion as a matter of tradition rather than personal conviction, or they have a sincere conviction but it is irrational and compartmentalized.

With the first type of individual, there's a simple answer to the question "How can an intelligent person believe in God?" They *don't*. They may go to church, wear a cross around their neck, and even have pictures of saints on their walls at home, but when it comes down to it, they don't really believe in what the church teaches—or even that God truly exists or has any kind of impact on their daily lives. They are what theologians call *nominal* Christians—believers in name only but not *true* believers.

Nominalism is a fairly widespread tendency, and as Ernest Renan, a nineteenth-century French philosopher and religious scholar observed, "Theological development has been quite null in France; there is no country in Europe where religious thought has been less active. . . . But as the need for a religion is one common to humanity, they find it convenient to take ready-made the system which lies handy, without stopping to consider whether it is acceptable."[11]

This partially explains why surveys on religion continually find that more than 50 percent of the French population claim to be Catholic, and only 30 percent profess to be atheists—and yet, when I was growing up, virtually everyone around me seemed to be as unconvinced about faith as I was.[12]

I do, however, understand some of the appeal: Despite my secular point of view, I still retained a vague feeling of belonging, of identifying with my family's religious tradition.

Faith and reason

The second reason I could imagine for why otherwise intelligent people might believe in the obviously absurd idea of God's existence is that they allow themselves an intellectual exemption in this area. It isn't so much a question of the truthfulness of their religious beliefs as it is an inclination to sidestep logical arguments when confronted with questions of faith. In other words, Christians may be intelligent, but they don't *use* their intelligence to shed light on their religious faith. Either they totally isolate their faith and don't think about it, or they think about it but allow themselves a certain amount of irrationality. Strangely enough, this type of circumvention is uniquely accepted in the area of religion. They would never tolerate it in any other realm of life.

At this point in my life, I was ignoring the existence of intelligent Christians—such as Augustine and Thomas Aquinas, to name just two—who did not set their faith aside in a logic-proof compartment. Moreover, the list of eminently qualified Christian thinkers boasts a fair number of Frenchmen, including John Calvin, René Descartes, Nicolas Malebranche, and Blaise Pascal. We can disagree with what these famous men say (and I do disagree with some of them on certain subjects), but they were clearly high-caliber theistic thinkers who had a profound influence in the realm of religion. Their works are recognized by atheist scholars as well as Christians, and they continue to influence the great contemporary philosophers who have come after them—which, in the English-speaking world today, would include the likes of Alvin Plantinga, Richard Swinburne, Peter van Inwagen, Paul Helm, and William Lane Craig, among hundreds of others. Are they mistaken about God? Maybe. Are they idiots or incapable of deep reflection? Certainly not. Have their minds gone off the rails on this one topic? Have their brains malfunctioned? It depends on what you believe about the purpose of the human brain. Alvin Plantinga, for one, has written a great deal about the "proper function" of our brains.[13]

According to a Christian worldview, the human brain was designed by God the Creator to allow us to think correctly and to come to the knowledge of truth, which also allows us to trust it.

According to Darwinian atheists, on the other hand, the human brain came into being through a long natural process, whereby we learned to reason in order to help us *survive*, not specifically to discover truth. We can believe whatever we want; natural selection doesn't really care about truth in itself. What matters is that our beliefs help us survive. This dilemma is what provoked Darwin's famous "horrid doubt":

> You have expressed my inward conviction, though far more vividly and clearly than I could have done, that the Universe is not the result of chance. But then with me the horrid doubt always arises whether the convictions of man's mind, which has been developed from the mind of the lower animals, are of any value or at all trustworthy. Would any one trust in the convictions of a monkey's mind, if there are any convictions in such a mind?[14]

In other words, there is no reason to think that if we reason well enough to survive, we will necessarily reason to produce true beliefs.[15]

A Darwinist and naturalist atheist should therefore doubt his own ability to know truth—and, by extension, doubt the trustworthiness of any belief produced by his own reasoning, including his own convictions about God and evolution. His position is self-refuting. It is quite literally irrational to believe it.[16]

An interesting response to this line of thinking comes from the French atheist philosopher André Comte-Sponville. In *The Little Book of Atheist Spirituality*, he attempts to refute some of the traditional arguments in favor of the existence of God. Some of these arguments are based on premises that are strongly supported by human reason; thus, to avoid the logical conclusion that God exists, Comte-Sponville attacks reason itself:

> Indeed, how can we be certain our reason is perfectly rational? Only a God could guarantee us that, and this is just what prevents our reason from proving his existence. It would be a vicious circle, as it is in Descartes: Our reason proves the existence of God, and God guarantees the veracity of our reason.[17]

He agrees, then, with Plantinga's claim that only God's existence guarantees us that our cognitive faculties are reliable; thus, to presuppose the reliability of our reason is to presuppose the existence of God. But because the arguments in favor of God's existence presuppose the reliability of our reason, Comte-Sponville accuses those arguments of presupposing the existence of the God they seek to prove!

This criticism, however, is misguided. Clearly, any rational argument in favor of God's existence presupposes the reliability of reason, but this reliability should not be called into question. It is recognized by everyone—atheist or Christian—who offers *any* rational argument.

Comte Sponville himself presupposes the reliability, or rationality, of human reason when he offers atheistic arguments in his book of atheist spirituality. If human reason is not reliable, why try to reason with his readers? Clearly he presupposes that human reason is reliable—and by adding that only a God can guarantee this, he's not offering us a reason to *doubt* God's existence; he's giving us a reason to *believe* it.

I didn't think of reason that way at the time; to me, if you employed reason, you would conclude that there is no God.

Relentless Pursuit
of Success

● ● ●

Nothing is worse than failure, except for
success when it does not fully satisfy.

LUC FERRY

IF YOU HAD TO BET on which kid in a group of young teenagers
would end up playing keyboards in a rock band, competing
on a championship-level volleyball team, and dating attractive young women, you probably wouldn't put your money
on a late-to-puberty straight-A student, with braces on his
teeth and enormous glasses, who spent his free time playing
video games and painting miniature models.

I wouldn't either.

When I started middle school, I wasn't exactly the most
happening kid in my class. I didn't have any close friends,
and I really wasn't looking for any, to be honest. It seemed
that the popular kids earned the admiration of others by

doing things that didn't interest me: disrespecting the teachers, smoking cigarettes or joints, listening to gangster rap, and dressing and acting like bad boys. It just wasn't my thing, so I never tried to belong to those groups.

On the other hand, I noticed that the popular boys attracted all the cute girls. So even though their behavior was repulsive to me, I wouldn't have minded being popular for a little while, if only for the girls.

Metamorphosis

Thanks to Maman's devotion to her children's well-being, I was involved in several sports from a young age. Over the years, I participated in gymnastics, tennis, handball, track and field, and badminton; but I never really excelled competitively until I discovered volleyball.

Nicolas had started playing a few years before I did, and he was on the city team in Montigny-Le-Bretonneux. One day, the club decided to replace their laid-back coach with a new guy, named Gilles, who turned out to be a fascinating person. Measuring somewhere around five foot four, which is short for a volleyball player, Gilles was an accomplished setter and an amazing technician on the court. Moreover, he was strong-willed, full of ambition, and his piercing voice filled the gym during practice. As Gilles imposed his will on the team, my brother and his teammates became really good players under his direction.

He also had an eye for potential.

One Sunday, when I was watching one of Nicolas's games, Gilles came up to see me in the bleachers. He introduced himself and said, "I want you to come play for me. Come in for a tryout."

I should probably mention that when puberty finally kicked in for me, it came with a vengeance. I grew almost eight inches in one summer, began devouring unbelievable quantities of food, and just kept growing. By the time I started high school, I had reached my adult height of six foot four.

I went to the next practice, just to see what was going on. It didn't take long to discover that volleyball was harder than Nicolas made it look. Nevertheless, Gilles took Nicolas and me aside after practice and said, "This year, I'm going to take this team to the selections for the junior varsity–level Coupe de France, and I want you to be on it, Guillaume."

What confidence! I had never touched a volleyball in my life, yet here was a topflight coach guaranteeing me a place on a team that would be playing high-level competition. His confidence and drive must have been contagious because I said yes.

Over the next few months, my teammates and I underwent brutal training, almost military style. I learned how many sets of push-ups my body could endure before collapsing. Gilles handed out a workout regimen—running, sit-ups, push-ups, sprints—like it was some kind of punishment for us but entertainment for him. Show up a couple minutes late for practice? Forty more push-ups. Dog it during a workout?

Run five laps around the gym. All of this could have discouraged us, but it had the opposite effect. We were a team of young men who were motivated to learn, and Gilles's coaching style helped us develop a rigorous sense of discipline, an excellent team spirit, and a strong competitive mindset. We competed in the selections for La Coupe de France, and we qualified! Even though we didn't win the cup itself, the games were exciting, and I was officially in love with the sport of volleyball. Gilles continued to coach us through the regular season, and I continued to improve, though somewhat slowly.

Until one day, during a summer volleyball camp, when Gilles took me aside and said, "Guillaume, I'm sick of this. With your height and your vertical leap, I don't understand why you're not better at offense. Come with me."

Gilles grabbed a cart filled with at least twenty volleyballs and took me to the net. As the other players sat down on the sidelines and watched in silence, the coach climbed up a ladder, held the first ball just above the net—at its regulation height of 7 feet 11⅝ inches—and said, "Okay, come on! Run, jump, and spike this ball with all your strength."

I did it, but the result wasn't all that impressive.

Gilles grabbed another ball. "Again!"

We repeated the exercise again and again and again, until the cart was empty.

"Go pick up all the balls!" Gilles shouted. And we started again.

Before long, I was completely exhausted, and my arms

were shaking. But then something amazing happened. As I took off running one more time, my legs pumping beneath me, my right arm rose to a height of about 10 feet 5 inches (my maximum reach at the time) and my hand came down on the ball with explosive power, driving it almost vertically into the three meter attack zone just beyond the net.

Boom!

"There you go!" Gilles shouted. "Do it again!"

I repeated the exercise ten more times, each time putting the ball away—with power—into the attack zone. I felt tears come to my eyes, and my teammates were speechless. In just a few minutes, I had been transformed from a tall but average frontline player into a particularly dangerous offensive weapon, capable of spiking the ball with authority.

During the following season, my brother and I continued to improve. Nicolas was in engineering school, and I was still in high school. We bought a bench and a set of weights and set them up in the garage. Every morning before school, we pumped iron, motivating each other to fight against our sore muscles. In a little over a year, I gained more than twenty pounds of muscle, and my vertical leap went through the roof.

Our team, Montigny-Le-Bretonneux, won several successive championships on a departmental, and then a regional, level. After a while, I decided to change teams to play at the national league level. I was still technically weak on defense, but I was bench-pressing 265 lbs, spiking at a height of 11 feet, and I had a jumping motion that kept me floating at that height for a particularly long time, which gave me a serious advantage on offense.

I loved the feeling of flying, even if just for a few seconds, before spiking the ball with all my strength to the sound of the crowd's applause. I received several offers from national-level teams and decided to play for Clamart—in part because several good friends of mine were on the team but also, to be honest, because the club was full of girls. Clamart boasted an excellent women's team that played in the pro league at the time, and many of the players were quite beautiful and athletic.

Indeed, my life was pretty much centered on girls at that point, and my physical metamorphosis allowed me to have much greater success than I'd had in junior high. I was finally tall and fit, my braces were gone, I wore contact lenses, and I kept my hair shorter—and I soon had some stories to contribute to the locker room banter.

"My little pianist"

During that same period, I started pursuing the piano more seriously as well. I had been playing since I was little, but I was finally starting to get excited about it. Through family connections, I had been blessed to learn the instrument from someone rather special. My aunt's brother was Claude Nougaro, a very famous French singer and songwriter. It was their mother, Liette Tellini (whom we called Mamoune), who had initially taught me how to play, using her own piano at her house in Paris. When I told my parents I wanted to continue taking lessons, they enrolled me in a classical piano class at a music school closer to home and took out a loan to buy me a beautiful, shiny black Yamaha upright. To this day, I thank God for my parents and their willingness to make sacrifices for my benefit.

I kept Mamoune abreast of my limited progress at the music school, but eventually I grew bored with classical piano and started taking private lessons at home from a teacher who gave me more modern pieces to play. My interest was rekindled for a while, but I wasn't very disciplined in my playing. It was only my mother's perseverance in making me practice between lessons that made the difference.

It wasn't until I discovered how cool playing keyboards could be that I got into it more seriously. I learned how to reproduce sounds on a synthesizer that resembled the metal rock bands I listened to. About this same time, my grandfather Dady decided to bequeath his twelve grandchildren a significant sum of money. My parents set aside half the money to pay for our college education and gave each of us our share of the other half.

My brother bought a motorcycle with his money, and I decided to put my half into a Kurzweil K2600X, the best professional keyboard on the market at the time. My piano playing talents didn't really warrant such a purchase, but I thought that buying a great keyboard might push me to excellence. The Kurzweil was a phenomenal instrument, with a graded hammer-action keyboard that felt like a real piano. It also had a faster return, which gave me the capacity for high-speed solos. In addition, there were all kinds of sound generators, organ simulators, and buttons for distortion and modulation.

I started playing and practicing for hours, even skipping school sometimes so I could spend more time practicing. With this highly disciplined approach to practice, I quickly began to improve—just like with my volleyball skills. After a while, I started playing in a band with my brother and some friends, but I soon joined another band started by one of my brother's childhood friends, who was an excellent technician on the guitar, along with his girlfriend, who was an amazing singer. We found a bass player and a drummer who possessed a breathtaking dexterity, and we hit the ground running, composing and recording our own music and playing concerts in local venues.

We never played in front of huge crowds, but in my eyes, we were still a success. We played our own compositions onstage, instead of covering songs from other bands, and it was good music, especially from a technical point of view. Although we never made it to the big time, we did have an opportunity to open a show for Superbus, a French pop/rock band that went on to sell 1.5 million records. I remember being exhausted but euphoric after that concert.

Success, but what's the point?

Opening for Superbus was the pinnacle of our band's achievements. I was twenty-four at the time, and the chain of events that would take me far from my native France was already in motion. But even though I had fulfilled my wildest childhood dreams, I found myself asking an unexpected question: "What's the point?"

I had achieved success in all the areas of my life that I valued. I was a straight-A student, now at L'Institut Supérieur d'Electronique de Paris, one of the more prestigious engineering schools in France. I was playing championship-level volleyball and living the dream of being a rock star on stage. On top of all that, after a string of relationships of varying lengths and levels of commitment, I was in a serious relationship with an amazing girl named Adèle—a tall, blonde, athletic, and charming volleyball player.

It seemed I had arrived, but I was asking myself, "What now? Is this happiness?" I wasn't even sure what happiness was. Now that I had achieved all my personal goals, was this all there was to life? My goals had been like a mountain to climb, but when I reached the summit, the view wasn't as exciting as I had anticipated. I wasn't unhappy or bored, but I kept asking myself, "What's the point?" without finding much of an answer.

I began to hope that someone with a bit more wisdom and experience might be able to shed some light on my elusive pursuit of happiness. I finally settled on the person I respected the most in my life, and whose own life had been an impressive example of amazing accomplishments: my grandpa Dady.

Dady earned his diploma at the École Polytechnique, one of France's most prestigious scientific and engineering universities. He spent his working days on the cutting edge of science—first, in researching chemical processes to treat gases and sulfur in industrial furnaces and, later, in an isotope separation plant, doing research in nuclear science. He established the separation process for uranium isotopes and was chief engineer at the outset of the project that made France a global nuclear power. His team was responsible for building the top-secret Pierrelatte uranium enrichment factory in the Drome region, and he helped build the ELF oil refinery at Grand-Puits before moving on to work at IBM France, where he created the first programs for the market's first powerful computers.

He survived two World Wars and was responsible for a territory the size of France in the Sahara Desert during World War II. The stories he tells of this period in his life are simply incredible. He speaks French, English, Arabic, and German fluently; can translate Latin; and is able to get by in Russian, Italian, Spanish, Greek, Hebrew, and Sanskrit. And believe it or not, as I write these words, Dady is 106 years old and still sharp as a tack.

As he was nearing his one hundredth birthday, Dady decided to write his autobiography—published only for the family—which I've read several times. Every time I pick it up, I find new and fascinating details about his remarkable life. So I figured if there was anyone who could tell me about happiness and how to live a full life, it would be Dady. Finally, I took up pen and paper (remember those?) and wrote him a letter.

Dear Dady,

*I know I don't write to you very often, and when
we have a chance to talk, it's usually about more
lighthearted subjects. But today I have a deeper question
to ask you: What is happiness? Over the past few years,
I have achieved most of my goals in different areas.
They all gave me a measure of temporary satisfaction,
but I don't know what to chase after anymore. Are you
happy with all that you accomplished in your long and
prosperous life? Do you feel that you have succeeded at
life? What can you tell me about the meaning of life
and the search for happiness?*

I mailed it off, and when Dady's reply finally arrived by
return mail, I read it carefully and with great anticipation.

Dear Guillaume, you've asked a difficult question . . .

Dady told me about some of the key moments in his
incredible life; times when he had experienced the deepest
contentment. His theory on happiness boiled down to this:
Happiness is a goal on the horizon that we can never reach,
and our most intensely joyful moments are only mile markers
to guide us on our path.

*We don't sit down at the mile marker, Guillaume; we
enjoy the moment and we move on.*

37

He proceeded to list some of his favorite mile markers. Several sounded impressive and exciting to me, such as the time he was in charge of a commando unit in the Sahara Desert and had to rely on his wits to get his team safely through a battle zone. He also made a couple of references to religion, mentioned a few Bible stories, and shared a moment in his own life when he had read Jesus' Sermon on the Mount to a group that had gathered on a mountainside in Israel—similar to the one where Jesus had spoken the same words two thousand years before. I didn't see a connection to my question about true happiness and the meaning of life, so I ignored the religious parts of the letter and focused on the rest.

It was a very personal and touching letter, but after reading it, I didn't feel much closer to an answer about the meaning of life. In my ignorance, I didn't see the obvious link between my questions and what Dady said about Jesus.

Why would he use religion to answer a question about life and happiness?

I would later discover that, as atheist philosopher Luc Ferry says, "Religion is irreplaceable as a source of meaning."[1] Indeed, God's existence is arguably *necessary* in order for life to have objective meaning.

The Creator and the objective of the game

As a good atheistic psychoanalyst, Sigmund Freud once declared, "When we begin to ask ourselves questions about the meaning of life and death, we are sick, for none of that exists objectively."[2]

I don't believe I was *sick* when I asked my grandpa those questions, but I believe Freud was right when he suggested that life has no objective meaning if God doesn't exist. Why not? Because only the Creator can determine the goal or objective of life. Without a purposeful creator, there is no objective. I know this well enough from my days playing volleyball.

Who decides the objective of the game of volleyball? That right goes to William G. Morgan, who invented the sport in 1895. Though some of the rules have been refined over the years, the objective has remained the same: ground the ball within the lines on the opponent's side of the net and keep the ball airborne on your own side of the net. If a player doesn't agree with Morgan's rules and prefers instead to juggle the ball and send it into the net while dancing a tango, that person is not playing volleyball. His or her idea of the game isn't just *different*; it is objectively *wrong*.

Now, if we remove the person who invented the game of volleyball and all its rules, we are left with a bunch of players in their team uniforms, standing around on the court. They have a ball and a net but no true purpose. No goal or objective is more valid than any other. If two players disagree on the objective of the game, one cannot claim to be *more right* than the other because neither player understands the purpose of the game as designed by the game's creator. Every player is free to choose a personal objective, but those are not the *true* objectives of the game.

Even if two teams agree on a goal for the game, it would still be a subjective goal, belonging to them alone, and it would be no more *valid* than any other contrary objective that two other teams might agree upon. Anyone is free to devise a game with a ball and a net and make up rules, but it wouldn't be *volleyball* because that game has already been created and already has rules and a fixed objective defined by its creator.

It's the same thing with the meaning of life on planet Earth. If God doesn't exist, then every human being can pursue their own personal goals, but those individual goals will never amount to *the meaning of life*. On the contrary, life would have no objective meaning. But if God *does* exist, and if God *did* create the universe, then he and he alone can define the objective, the goal, and the governing rules of life.

When we seek for the *meaning* of something, writes Luc Ferry, "one can posit the following axiom: Anything that is not the effect of a will, . . . anything that is not in some way the manifestation of a subjectivity, has no meaning, makes no sense. . . . For meaning exists only in a relation of one person to another, in the bond that unites two wills, whether or not we think of them as purely human."[3]

For believers in God the Creator, he is the "person" who is the source of life's meaning. What is the meaning of life according to Christianity? Various Christian thinkers may phrase it in different ways, but one way or another it will have to do with bringing glory to God.[4] And one obvious way we can glorify God is to love him.[5] And a

Christian's love for God naturally and necessarily includes the way he or she treats other people. Jesus made a close connection between the two dimensions when he said, "Love the Lord your God with all your heart and . . . love your neighbor as yourself."[6]

Luc Ferry tries to defend an atheistic philosophy that retains from Christianity its ultimate foundation of love as the meaning of life.[7] But if there is no Creator God who has a *goal* or *design* for his creation, no God who guarantees that life has some objective meaning, how can we say that loving others is the meaning of life? Why not say that the meaning of life is accumulating riches, vying for power, seeking personal glory, taking a nap, or anything else we might choose? The choice is arbitrary and subjective.

Do you disagree with Luc Ferry? Great! In the absence of a Creator God, your opinion is worth just as much as his.

This was my dilemma: I was seeking happiness and the meaning of life while, at the same time, excluding the source of meaning by rejecting God. What could I do then, once I had achieved all my personal goals without ever finding full satisfaction? Augustine prayed, "Thou hast made us for thyself and restless is our heart until it comes to rest in thee."[8] By definition, my heart could not find that rest. Similarly, the author of the Old Testament book of Ecclesiastes affirms that God has "planted eternity in the human heart."[9] Eternity is arguably another necessary condition for a meaningful life, and it, too, was excluded from my worldview.

Eternal life and ultimate meaning

Eternity is necessary to give life an ultimate meaning, because if there is nothing after we die, then death results in an inevitable and universal annihilation. If death is the end of all things, it is the Great Eraser that cancels out any impact we made with our lives and removes all meaning from our existence. What's the difference between one path and another in this world if all we're destined for is destruction? In such a scenario, anything we do in life is tantamount to building a house on a hillside where an avalanche is coming. It's an exercise in futility because the house will soon be crushed and disappear beneath the snow.

Many French atheist philosophers recognize this consequence and tend to affirm it explicitly. Renowned religious historian Ernest Renan doesn't like the traditional Christian view of eternal life, yet he wants to rescue some form of eternity to affirm the beauty/meaningfulness of the world. "As soon as we deny immortality in an absolute manner," he writes, "the world becomes colorless and sad."[10]

Philosopher Albert Camus had a similar take on the absurdity of life without God, suggesting that the only philosophical question worth asking is whether to commit suicide.[11] Baron d'Holbach was just as explicit when he observed that "death appears to the wretched the only remedy for despair."[12]

Many atheists who reflect on the questions of death and the meaning of life seem to come to the same conclusion: Without God and without eternity, life has no meaning.

André Comte-Sponville offers us this straightforward conclusion: "In a word, Pascal, Kant, and Kierkegaard were
right: There is no way for a lucid atheist to avoid despair."[13]

Personally, I wasn't interested in a life filled with despair,
so I naturally did what Blaise Pascal suggested three and
a half centuries ago: "Men, unable to remedy death, sor-
row, and ignorance, determine, in order to make themselves
happy, not to think on these things."[14] I stopped thinking
about these things and went on with my life. Without asking myself the deeper questions, I continued with my self-
centered activities and sought for happiness—sometimes
(perhaps often) at the expense of other people.

4

Happiness at Any Price

• • •

In nature, there cannot be either confusion, or real evil,
since everything follows the laws of its natural existence.

BARON D'HOLBACH

SETTING ASIDE THE PHILOSOPHICAL QUESTIONS for the moment,
I thought I pretty much had it made. I had finished my
engineering studies and found a promising job as a software
developer for a consulting company that placed me at a
major French bank only five minutes away by car. Throw in
volleyball, music, and women, and I had just about everything I wanted from life. And I had done it all honestly.
Well, at least I had never stolen anything . . . um, let's just
say I've never done anything illegal—anything that would be
punishable by law.

In my studies, I avoided cheating on (almost) all my exams.
In volleyball, I never went in for doping, unless you count

sweetened condensed milk. And unlike many of my team-mates, I never got involved with drugs. Despite a good dose of pride about my music, I didn't have much opportunity for great evil there, either. Not all my compositions were 100 percent original, but I never plagiarized anyone else's work. However, when it came to my relationships with women, I clearly broke another type of law—a moral one—in my search for happiness. But I wasn't thinking in those terms at the time.

In my blind obsession with pursuing my own satisfaction, I caused a great deal of pain. And even though my moral code at the time was fairly loose, I wasn't always proud of myself. I didn't lose much sleep dwelling on the emotional havoc I caused, but as I pursued my conquests, I broke more than a few laws in the mysterious code of a man's moral duty toward women.

A romantic catastrophe

Four years before I met Adèle, I was in a long-term relationship with a brunette named Laetitia, whom I had met at the beginning of my university studies. Things weren't great from the very start. I was initially interested in her older sister, Coralie, and I invited Coralie to spend an afternoon with me to see if I wanted to date her. A few weeks later, I asked her to a movie, and Laetitia came along. She was two years younger than Coralie, and I found her even more attractive than her older sister. Wanting to keep my options open, I picked them up from the train with two roses—one for each girl. Later, in the dark movie theater, I took Laetitia's hand, and when I walked the sisters back to the train station, I kissed Laetitia right in front of Coralie! Not the classiest way to start. But Laetitia and I got past our bumpy beginnings and had something of a long-term relationship.

Laetitia lived an hour away by train, so we saw each other only on weekends. We didn't have much in common, so we spent most of our time at the movies, listening to music, or having sex. The intense feelings I had for her at first began to dwindle over time, and I started cheating on her with one-night stands. After months of lying to Laetitia, I ended up confessing to her. Confronted with her hurt and anger, I found I didn't have much motivation to work things out, and we soon broke up.

Not long afterward, while I was still looking for another relationship after Laetitia, I heard she was going out with one of my best friends, Alessandro, who lived across the street from me. Even though I had cheated on her and broken up with her, my pride was wounded. (Just to give you an idea of how disturbed my thinking was.)

Around the same time, I visited a friend of my brother's in Paris, who wanted to set me up with her roommate. I spent the evening with the two girls but felt the roommate was somewhat reserved. Still, at the end of the evening, I found myself in her bed. But just as things were heating up, she put on the brakes. She said she had been badly hurt in her last relationship and she wanted to take things slow and build something serious and lasting. That was the very opposite of what I wanted. Lying there in the dark, I reassured her of my noble intentions, and she finally let me have my way. Then, in the early morning hours, I crept out of bed, slipped out of the apartment, and never saw her again.

I still thought of myself as a pretty good guy in general, but I felt really guilty after leaving like that. As I was fleeing the scene, I told myself I should never do that again.

With my self-esteem at an all-time low, I went to see Laetitia and laid my heart on the line. My seductive charm must have worked because she broke up with Alessandro and came back to me. Of course, my friendship with Alessandro was destroyed—which I still regret to this day. He had been a sincere and true friend, and he deserved better.

To make matters worse, my relationship with Laetitia was going nowhere. With all the water under the bridge, our situation was a lot more complicated now. She was no longer the joyful girl I had first met, and I soon grew tired of her again. I thought about breaking up once and for all, but I couldn't muster the courage to go through with it. I knew it would break her heart again, and I'd have to put up with more tears. And to be honest, I didn't want to be unattached again. I needed to find someone to give me the motivation to go through with it. That's when I met Adèle.

The beauty of a clean slate

Adèle was on the women's volleyball team, and we practiced in the same gym but on different courts. I had noticed her from afar and thought she was magnificent even though we had never spoken to each other. Someone introduced us during a sporting event, and I found she was as beautiful up close as she was from afar. She had a great personality and we talked a lot that day, even flirted some. Throughout the week, we kept in touch through text messages.

That weekend, as usual, Laetitia came to spend Saturday afternoon with me. As we were lying on my bed together watching a movie, I was secretly texting Adèle. Our messages became more and more intimate, and Adèle ended up admitting she had feelings for me.

Laetitia was understandably irritated by my silence and my rapt attention to my phone. You could cut the tension with a knife, and I used the uncomfortable silence as a pretext. When it was time for her to leave, I drove her to the railway station and practically dumped her at the platform—leaving all her tears for her seatmates on the train. Without even looking back, I got into my car and drove over to Adèle's. (I know, what a gentleman.)

The one downside to my relationship with Adèle, which had previously escaped my notice, was that she had just come out of a serious relationship with one of my best friends on the volleyball team, Pierre-Olivier. The thought of asking my friend how he would feel about my dating his ex-girlfriend never crossed my mind. But it should have. After all, Adèle and I were aware enough that we started going out in secret.

Despite our attempted discretion, Pierre-Olivier caught us one afternoon during a surprise visit to Adèle, and he was deeply hurt and offended by my backstabbing. For the second time in just a few months, I had demolished a close friendship because of a girl.

I should mention that Pierre-Olivier was also the new coach of my team in Montigny. (Gilles had left and I had not yet started playing at the national level.) He had taught me so much and had given me a great spot on the team. And I knew he had made personal sacrifices for me several times. Once, when I had been going through a hard time with Laetitia, he and his family invited me to go on vacation with them to the French Riviera. In a word, he was the perfect friend. And here I was, putting my personal interests above his without a second thought. He obviously still had feelings for Adèle, but none of that mattered to me. The only thing I cared about was that she was beautiful and charming and I was certain she would make me happy. Too bad for everyone else.

The moral of the story

I thought I had finally found happiness, though it came at the expense of women I hurt deeply and good friends I betrayed. But I was so blinded by my desire for happiness that I wasn't convinced I had done anything wrong. I told myself the ends justified the means, and there was no law against what I had done.

What's interesting to me, in retrospect, is that my pursuit of happiness at any cost brought me closer to facing the question of God's existence, though I wanted nothing to do with it at the time. Indeed, for many Christian thinkers, human morality is one of the great signs of God's existence. The connection between God and morality can be seen when you ask yourself an essential question about good and evil: Was what I did objectively *wrong*, or was it simply a matter of personal preference?

Traditionally, Christians have based morality (the difference between good and evil) on God's nature and his commandments: do not commit murder, do not lie, do not commit adultery, love your neighbor as yourself, etc. If God is the creator of the universe and all it contains, including the human race, we are morally obligated to obey his commandments. According to a theistic view of morality, there is an *objective* difference between good and evil. That is, it is objectively *good* to love my neighbor and objectively *evil* to rape someone, torture a child, or take what isn't mine. Whether or not I agree, if God is the creator of the universe, morality is not a matter of personal preference; it is a matter of objective truth. Good is good. Evil is evil.

On the other hand, if God does not exist, morality arguably becomes *subjective*. There is no basis on which to say that any point of view is ultimately right or that one person's opinion is worth more than another's. André Comte-Sponville highlights this point, drawing on the teachings of Immanuel Kant:

> To have a religion, the *Critique of Practical Reason* points out, is to "acknowledge all one's duties as sacred commandments." For those who no longer

have faith, commandments vanish (or, rather, lose their sacred quality), and all that remains are duties—that is, the commandments we impose upon ourselves.[1]

Who is this "we" that Comte-Sponville speaks of? It is each of us as individuals, and all of society. But in the absence of a sacred, objective standard, these personal impositions are merely subjective; thus, they cannot be imposed upon my neighbor. If my neighbor is a sociopath, who by nature imposes far fewer restrictions on himself than others do, nothing and no one can objectively decide between his point of view and mine. Moral commandments are based merely on each person's or each society's preferences. I may feel extremely passionate about the commandments I impose upon myself, but my preferences are no *truer* than anyone else's. If, on the contrary, not all moral judgments are subjective, if some things truly are right and wrong, then it would follow that God exists.

So how did I avoid this conclusion during my years as an atheist? It's hard to say. I didn't think in those terms because no one had ever presented me with this explicit argument. My guilty conscience simply reminded me from time to time that I was behaving badly.

In this context, I think I would have said that the *pain* I caused was objective, because it certainly felt real to me. But I never asked myself why I had a guilty conscience in the first place; whether there were moral rules independent of my own feelings or opinion. I preferred not to think about it. Competitive volleyball, playing in a rock band, my beautiful girlfriend—everything was as it should be, and life was good. What more could I ask for? What could possibly go wrong?

That question was soon answered when Adèle left me.

I was crushed, but I consoled myself for a brief time in the arms of Emma, a blonde-haired, blue-eyed Brit who was taking some classes in Paris for her college degree. Because I wasn't expecting a long-term commitment from her, I was able to say goodbye a few weeks later when she decided she wanted to spend more time with me and thought I was too wrapped up in all my activities: work, volleyball, and music. No problem. She had provided temporary comfort, and I had renewed confidence in my ability to charm women.

At the same time, I had recently purchased a one-bedroom apartment about fifteen minutes from work and home, and at the tender age of twenty-four, I was discovering the freedom of no longer living with my parents. Despite a few bumps in the road, my life was shaping up to be all that I wanted it to be. Though I was back to square one in my search for the perfect woman, the timing was great because it was almost July, and Nicolas and I had plans for a three-and-a-half-week vacation to the sunny Caribbean island of Saint Martin.

5

The Turning Point

• • •

This is my manner of acting: in the village I go to
mass; in the town I laugh at those who go there.

ERNEST RENAN

AS SOON AS I RETURNED HOME from Saint Martin— tanned,
relaxed, and ready for whatever would come next—Vanessa
and I began planning for her to come visit me. We settled
on October—after she had accrued enough vacation days
again and before my next volleyball season began. Any later
and all my weekends would be busy. In the meantime, there
I was, living in Paris, while my beautiful new girlfriend was
on the far side of the Atlantic. In some ways, it didn't matter
because her religious beliefs would have kept us from sleeping together even if she had been living in the apartment
next door.

What a drag!

I decided there was only one thing to do: I had to convince her that her religious convictions were unfounded so she would give up her illogical beliefs and we could live happily ever after.

As I contemplated this challenge, I realized I had *no idea* what she even believed. She had told me she was a Christian, but I wasn't exactly sure what that meant. From my vague memories of catechism class, I knew she had to be either Catholic, Protestant, or Orthodox—and I was pretty certain she wasn't Catholic. When I asked her which one she was, she had said, "None of the above; just Christian." I thought that was a strange answer, and I was very confused.

I rooted through my closet and found a dusty old Bible that obviously hadn't been opened in years. Rubbing the cover like it was Aladdin's lamp, I read the title: *Traduction Ecuménique de la Bible* (*Ecumenical Translation of the Bible*). Here was another word I didn't understand: *écuménique*. Out of curiosity, I opened the Bible to see what was in it.

I soon realized I had no idea what this book contained despite years of attending Mass and sitting in catechism classes where I was supposed to be learning about it. It didn't matter; Vanessa and I would talk about this nonsense the next time we were together.

Paris

As Vanessa prepared to fly to France, she asked me to help her resist sexual temptation while she was with me.

No way! I told her the first thing I was going to do was break down her resistance.

She didn't like my answer, but what could she say? If her religion preached abstinence before marriage, why was she putting herself in a situation where she'd be sleeping in the same apartment as a young French atheist who was under her spell?

Still, she came for a visit.

On her first evening in Paris, I had volleyball practice and couldn't miss it. She decided to stay at my apartment and rest from her trip while I went to Clamart.

Before I left, she took some presents out of her suitcase, including some old modeling flyers filled with gorgeous pictures of her. I stuck one in my gym bag, and when I got to the locker room, I bragged, "Hey, guys, look what's waiting for me at home!"

My comments gave the impression that a steamy evening awaited me after practice; but honestly, I wasn't sure I could get Vanessa to give in. As it turned out, she stuck fast to her convictions, and we didn't sleep together.

She seemed really serious about her values, and I asked myself what would happen if she wasn't willing to give them up. Resisting sex before marriage seemed like a superhuman feat to me; but even beyond that, could I stand her going to church every Sunday? Worst case scenario, she could go alone, but I knew it would bother me to see her spend so much time there. And how would we raise our kids?

Two other things made me realize how serious she was about her religion. First, her pastor in New York had taken her to the airport, and he would be picking her up when she got home. Warning bells went off in my head, and I began to wonder if she was part of some cult like I had seen in TV documentaries. Second, she had emailed a friend, asking her to send the address of a church in Paris, just in case we might attend on Sunday morning while she was here. Couldn't she even take a break for two weekends and spend her Sundays quietly at home with me? This bothered me, and it was clear we would have to seriously negotiate the terms of her beliefs.

While we were enjoying a delicious French meal at a restaurant in Montmartre, I broached the subject. I wanted to ask her if she was ready to give up her silly religion, but I decided to go at it more delicately. I thought it might make her more open to my suggestion.

"Vanessa, we need to talk about something. If we get married one day, are you ready to accept the fact that I'm an atheist?"

When I asked the question, I thought it would be the beginning of a long, intimate conversation. I told her that she could take her time about answering and we could talk about it later.

"Oh, no!" she said. "The answer is very simple. The answer is *no*, I can't."

What? Her reply—so innocent, so immediate, so unequivocal—echoed in my head.

Here I was, almost ready to make the sacrifice of letting her believe whatever she wanted—and letting her go to church on Sundays!—and she wasn't even willing to accept that I might disagree with her beliefs?

How intolerant!

Moreover, if her answer was so obvious, why hadn't she told me before? That would have kept us from planning what was now an absurd Parisian vacation together.

In my eyes, religion was a deal breaker.

Seeing that I was upset, she accepted my offer to talk more about the subject when we got home. The rest of the evening was enjoyable enough, but there was definitely tension in the air.

When we got back to my apartment, I said, "It seems unlikely that we'll have a future together."

My brutally honest declaration clearly took Vanessa by surprise. She looked at me sadly and said, "I don't understand how you can be so negative about this. Are you so narrow-minded that you can't even honestly consider the subject? You haven't even asked me what I believe!"

Her words caught me off guard. She was right. I hadn't asked her anything about her beliefs. I stood with my mouth open, trying to gather my thoughts. I didn't have an answer for her. I had to admit that I was being narrow-minded. After a few moments of silence, I reluctantly conceded the point.

"You're right. The least I can do is ask you what you believe. Go ahead, tell me everything. I'm listening."

She sat down next to me on the couch and told me a story about her life and conversion that was so completely crazy to me that—even today—I'm not sure I believe all the details. I'll give you the short version.

Modeling, mafiosi, and mom

Vanessa had grown up in Florida, but she left home at the age of thirteen to become an actress and a model. Her career took off right away, but a few years later, she found herself mixed up with a guy who had some very shady dealings and even shadier connections.

She said her boyfriend beat her and threatened her life on a regular basis, and he had several run-ins with the police. Eventually, they moved to New York, but the job she was pursuing there fell through and she ended up working for her boyfriend. She cut off all contact with her family—believing it was for their protection—and became a prisoner in her own home, constantly battling depression.

One day, when her boyfriend left on a business trip, she decided to end her life. In the middle of her suicide attempt, as she was lying on the floor, someone came into the house and saved her life.

It was her mother.

Apparently, her mother had recently become a Christian and had "heard God speaking to her," telling her to go to New York and find Vanessa. She saved her daughter's life, preached the gospel to her, and Vanessa became a Christian that day.

With her mother's help, Vanessa escaped from her boyfriend and secretly moved to the other side of New York, renting an apartment under an assumed name and starting over with a new job in a legitimate company.

From everything she told me—and there was a lot that was hard to fathom—it was obvious she believed not only in God but also in divine intervention. But her story didn't do much to convince me of God's existence. In order to reach a conclusion for myself, I knew I would have to look into Christianity on my own—to apply some logic and reason to the subject. I decided I would begin my investigation as soon as Vanessa left Paris.

Reading the Bible

If I wanted to refute Christianity, I needed to know what its claims were. I opened the *Ecumenical Translation of the Bible* and started reading the New Testament, starting with the Gospels, which tell the story of the life and death of Jesus.

Before I began, I looked up the definition of *ecumenical* and found it meant a collaboration between Catholics, Protestants, and Orthodox Christians. I liked the idea that this translation of the Bible seemed neutral in its approach. Perhaps it would be balanced by disagreements on all sides so that one religious tradition would not hold sway over the others. The idea of objectivity was important to me from the start. After all, I was considering something that had enormous implications for my life.

From the outset, I had to force myself to be open-minded for the sake of intellectual honesty because I really wanted everything to be false. On the other hand, if I hoped to build a life with Vanessa, and if she proved impossible to convince otherwise about her faith, I realized I could be drawn the other way, wanting things to be true just to make it work with Vanessa.

There was danger in partiality from both sides, though neither one canceled out the other. I had to do everything in my power so that neither my desire to disprove Christianity nor my desire to be with Vanessa would determine the outcome of my investigation. Clearly, neither desire was a legitimate standard for evaluating the truth. I couldn't get *rid* of my desires (who can?), but I could do my best to weigh the questions objectively, regardless of my personal biases.

It was with this mindset that I started reading the Bible. But first, I mustered some of that open-mindedness I was aiming for by doing something I had never done before: I attempted an unbelieving prayer, as an atheist.

I don't know if there's a God up there somewhere; I don't believe so. But since I'm trying this out, here we go: God, if you exist, you might be interested in my investigation. So go ahead, reveal yourself to me, my mind is open.

Well, my mind wasn't really all that open, but I told myself that if God in fact existed, my unbelief wouldn't stop him. I embarked upon reading the Gospels over the next few weeks, in the spare time I had between work, volleyball practice, and playing with my band.

A little light reading

As I read the Bible for the first time, I was surprised by what I found. I had expected to read a series of boring platitudes, like those I had heard on Sundays in church as a child. But I discovered, to the contrary, that Jesus was a unique and fascinating character. I was especially intrigued by the masterful way he navigated conversations despite the hostility of others. He was constantly in conflict with the religious leaders, and he criticized them much more pointedly than he did the sinners. But when those leaders tried to ensnare him publicly, his answers always left them speechless.[1]

Jesus spoke of the "Kingdom of God" and taught with such wisdom that the crowds wondered how someone with no formal education could know such things.[2] He taught with such a sense of divine authority and proclaimed himself as the Messiah announced in the Old Testament,[3] the only Son of God—"the way, and the truth, and the life."[4] He invited the Jews to believe in him in the same way they believed in God[5] because no one could come to God without going through him.[6] He announced that he had come to save the world,[7] and everyone who entrusted their life to Jesus would save it.[8]

I didn't know what to do with this Jesus. He was full of wisdom and quick comebacks, and he proclaimed his supreme authority while being humble enough to wash his disciples' dirty feet.[9] He announced that he hadn't come to be served but to serve and "to give his life as a ransom for many."[10] There was no room in my worldview for his teachings about God and his claims of performing miracles, but one thing was certain: He was a fascinating person. And no matter what I might think about him, he spoke with authority and seemed to know what he was doing. His incisive manner made me uncomfortable, and I realized that, sooner or later, I'd have to decide who Jesus really was. However, at this point, I was still far from being ready to accept religion, and I couldn't have attended church if I'd wanted to because I had volleyball games every weekend all over France.

But that barrier didn't last long.

A visit to the zoo

Several weeks after my unbelieving prayer and the beginning of my investigation of Christianity, I started having serious pain in my right shoulder. Just like that, with no explanation and no apparent cause, my shoulder just gave out on me. It started about fifteen minutes into each practice, rendering me incapable of spiking the ball or even lifting my arm after warm-ups.

Over the next several weeks, I had recurrent inflammation in my shoulder joint. The doctor couldn't find anything wrong, and the physical therapist wasn't able to help me. They finally told me, "Guillaume, we can't figure this out. You probably just need to rest your shoulder. No more volleyball for a few weeks."

Suddenly, and against my will, I was off the team—and free on weekends—for the foreseeable future.

The next Sunday, I decided to make the most of the situation and finally satisfy my curiosity about these Christians that Vanessa claimed to be part of. I decided to go see them up close and personal. The email from her friend was still on my computer, so I was able to look up the church's address without her knowing. Then I mustered all my courage, jumped into my car, and headed for the gate of Saint-Ouen at the northern border of Paris.

Fortunately, since I had my own place now, I was able to undertake this exploratory venture without anyone else becoming aware. If I had still been living at home with my family, I never could have explained to my parents why I—Guillaume—was going out early on a Sunday to meet with a bunch of Christians.

In all honesty, I went to the church like someone would go to the zoo: to see exotic animals he had heard of but never actually seen.

When I arrived, I parked my car in front of the church building and headed haltingly toward the door, pausing to read a plaque on the side of the building: "Evangelical Protestant Church."

Aha! I knew it! I knew she was a Protestant!

I didn't know what that meant in practice, but it was

something Vanessa and I could talk about later. For now, I just needed to open the door.

I entered the church as quietly as I could. It was a modern building without arches or stained glass windows. Up front stood a podium, a couple of amplifiers, and a drum set. There were no church pews, just a hundred chairs or so. Everywhere I looked, people were standing around talking. I slipped in discreetly, hoping no one would notice me. I was very uncomfortable, and I couldn't stop thinking that if anyone from my family or my friends had seen me at that moment— in a *church*—I would have died of embarrassment. These thoughts were quickly interrupted by a smiling young man, probably from the French West Indies, who approached me.

Oh, no! What does he want?

"Hey, my name is David. If you want to come over here with us, we're going to pray together before the service."

Wow, I guess my plan to be invisible didn't work!

Obviously, I wasn't going to pray with them, but why not see what they're up to? Six or seven young adults were standing in a circle with their heads bowed. They began to pray aloud, taking turns, yet they weren't reciting prayers they had memorized. They spoke freely and with great affection: "God my Father," and this and that . . . "Lord Jesus, draw near to us," and so on.

Interesting. They all seemed to believe they were speaking to a God who was listening. Strange. I stood there, straight as an arrow, without making a sound.

If I'm really quiet, maybe they'll forget I'm here.

They finished praying as the music began, signaling the beginning of the service. I stepped away from the group and sat down off to the side yet close enough to the front to be able to observe and hear everything. The band was playing an upbeat song (a far cry from the old organ music of my childhood church). I noticed that David was the bass player.

Wow! He's a great bassist; he must be a professional musician. And, hey, the pianist/lead singer is really good too. What a powerful voice!

As a musician myself, I recognized and appreciated their talent.

Once the singing was over, the pastor picked up the microphone. He was about my dad's age and seemed intelligent and articulate. He spoke perfect French but with an American accent. He moved around the podium at a leisurely pace, with what seemed to be a sincere smile.

I promise you that I listened to him, but I don't remember a single word he said. Maybe I just wasn't able to absorb the message or was too self-conscious about being there, but I got absolutely nothing out of the sermon.

The service ended with another time of singing, and I told myself to get out of there before anyone else came to talk to me. I had seen what I wanted to see, and now it was time to go. Quickly, I rose and walked rapidly down the middle aisle toward the door, careful not to make eye contact with anyone.

When I reached the exit and began to step outside, I was suddenly overcome with a wave of chills that traveled up from my stomach and into my chest before taking hold of my throat. I stopped in my tracks, halfway out the door, my body covered with goosebumps.

This is ridiculous, I thought. *I need to understand.*

Just as quickly as I had fled up the aisle, I turned around, shut the door, and walked straight back to the pastor.

"Hi, my name is Guillaume," I said abruptly.

"Robert Baxter. Nice to meet you," he replied, still smiling and now looking a bit curious.

"So you believe in God, huh?"

"Yes," he said with a bemused smile.

"Well, how does that work?"

He told me he'd be happy to talk to me about it if I would be interested in setting up a meeting. He gave me his contact information but appeared doubtful that this impatient young man with the brusque manner would come back to hear about God.

Intellectual Barriers

• • •

Sensible men have the greatest advantage in
examining opinions, which it is pretended must
have an influence over their eternal happiness.

BARON D'HOLBACH

"GOOD EVENING. My name is Guillaume and I have a seven
o'clock appointment with Pastor Robert."

"Oh, yes, his office is right down the hall. Go on in; the
door is open."

"Thank you."

Approaching the pastor's door, I knocked lightly to let
him know I was there.

"Hey, good evening!" he said, rising from his desk and
coming to greet me.

The office was simply but comfortably furnished, and
the desk was littered with books and papers. Pastor Robert
invited me to take a seat on a sofa at the far end of the room.
He sat down in an armchair across from me, on the other side

of a small end table. I don't remember what we talked about at the beginning of our conversation, but Pastor Robert was friendly and warm. He asked me if he could pray for me before we got started.

"Uh, sure . . ."

He prayed aloud for me, and I felt as strange as I had on Sunday at the church service. At the same time, I found it reassuring that he seemed to really believe what he preached.

When he finished his prayer, I began to explain the reason for my visit.

Robert listened to me patiently and asked a lot of questions. We talked for a long, long time. So long, in fact, that I forgot about dinner. Robert expressed himself calmly, explained his ideas clearly, and it was truly a pleasure to talk with him. He was obviously an educated man, very intelligent, and he *really* believed in the existence of God, that Jesus was the Son of God, and that Jesus had been crucified and then raised from the dead.

My curiosity was definitely piqued. I wanted to test Robert's strange ideas, so I continued to ask questions and found myself caught up in his answers.

Despite our lengthy conversation that evening, I still wasn't satisfied. I had a lot more questions about the Christian faith. We decided to get together again soon.

As I was leaving, Robert handed me a little booklet he had written. It was a large list of questions on the basics of Christianity, and there were Bible verses to look up so I could find the answers myself.

As soon as I got back to my apartment, I opened my Bible and dove into the booklet. As I found answers to the questions, I wrote them on a sheet of paper. But every time I found an answer, it raised another question in my mind. I began to scribble notes in the margins of the paper, and that first sheet quickly became a pile of notes listing question after question I intended to ask Robert at our next appointment.

I returned to his office for another session, and then another. Soon we were getting together regularly. Over the next few months, we met to discuss God and major life issues. Our conversations were always cordial, though at times they felt more like a debate than a discussion. But they were never boring.

Little by little, my talks with Robert began to change my way of thinking about a number of things. In fact, partly due to Robert's explanations and partly due to my own research, I discovered that my perspective on several issues had been wrong. I suppose that's bound to happen sometimes when we reflect honestly on what we believe and why we believe it—and when we seriously consider opposing ideas. I eventually came to wrestle with several important facts, which triggered changes in my beliefs in five main areas: the supernatural, science, sex, knowledge, and salvation.

A sensible man who believes in miracles?

From the first time Robert and I met, and even before he answered any of my questions about Christianity, I was confronted with a bothersome truth: Apparently, it was possible to be rational and yet believe in the existence of God. Here was a sensible, well-educated, and intelligent man affirming his belief in miracles and the supernatural—beliefs I had always assumed were the realm of weak souls and naïve people who were easily taken in by charlatans.

Of course, being sensible didn't mean he had studied the questions in depth or that his reasons for believing in the supernatural were *good* reasons, but it did suggest that one didn't have to be stupid or mentally ill to believe in such things.

You might ask who in their right mind would say that all believers are either stupid or mentally ill. Well, I can point to the famous French historian and philosopher Ernest Renan as one example. In his book *The Future of Science*, Renan asserts that any belief in the supernatural is a kind of "strange malady," of the same order as magic or witchcraft.[1]

As I spent time with Robert, this naïve view began to crumble before my eyes. Upon further reflection, I saw that belief in the supernatural didn't have to be as extravagant as magic or witchcraft. All Robert was affirming was that *something* existed beyond the visible realm—that is, beyond the realm of matter in motion under the influence of the laws of nature. Was that really so unbelievable?

According to Robert's way of thinking, there was something outside or beyond the natural world. God and miracles would certainly fall into this category. But even Luc Ferry, a confirmed atheist, supports this idea when he says that certain concepts that are quite real (such as free will or moral values) transcend nature.[2] It goes without saying that Luc Ferry isn't an idiot, any more than Robert was.

Others may argue that it shouldn't be earthshaking news to discover that intelligent people believe in the supernatural. It shouldn't have been for me, in any case, because both my father and grandfather professed to believe in God. But the difference between them and Robert was that he believed in the supernatural with all his heart, and God was central to his life. This was, of course, obvious from the profession he chose, but it had also been the case before he became a pastor. He told me the story of his conversion to Christianity and how a sort of "waking vision" had led him straight to Jesus.

It was still strange to me, and certainly unusual, but I slowly came to accept that belief in the supernatural wasn't necessarily irrational. Or at least it wasn't a form of intellectual suicide. Just because an idea isn't widely accepted in modern culture doesn't mean it's unquestionably silly.

As I came to grips with the prospect of the supernatural, I began to realize that I also had to grapple with another tenet of Christianity—one that was absolutely unacceptable in my circle of French culture: *abstinence before marriage*. I needed to straightforwardly address what I believed about sex even more than what I believed about miracles.

Marriage, sex, and intimacy

The way I saw things at the time, Vanessa held two problematic beliefs about marriage. One was that marriage was the only morally acceptable framework for sex; and the other was that a Christian should not marry a non-Christian. The first of these beliefs seemed repressive and old-fashioned to me, and the second just seemed intolerant. So I asked Robert several pointed questions, hoping his answers would help me better understand what Christianity had to say on the subject and see if he could defend his point of view.

Before he could answer my questions, he said, he first had to clarify the biblical view of sexuality and distinguish it from some of its grotesque caricatures, which are often propagated in our modern world, and which I found daunting. We often hear that Christianity implies a hatred of sex. Michel Onfray openly advances this view when he associates the three main monotheistic religions with "hatred of sexuality, women, and pleasure; hatred of the feminine; hatred of the body, of desires, of drives."[3] Onfray later repeats that Christianity implies a hatred for the body, passions, women, love, and sex,[4] "to which might be added hatred of everything women represent for men: desire, pleasure, life."[5]

Robert helped me see that Onfray's claim is complete nonsense. On the contrary, he said, the Bible affirms that sexuality is a *gift* from our Creator, who invites us to "be fruitful and multiply" on the earth.[6] In the New Testament, the apostle Paul instructs spouses not to refrain from sexual intimacy, except for a limited time on which they both agree (for example, a specific time of prayer), and afterward to join together again in sexual union.[7] The Song of Solomon, in the Hebrew Bible, is a poem filled with illustrations, some very explicit, about the joy and pleasure that spouses take in the beauty of each other's body. The book of Proverbs tells us explicitly: "Let your wife be a fountain of blessing for you. Rejoice in the wife of your youth. She is a loving deer, a graceful doe. Let her breasts satisfy you always. May you always be captivated by her love."[8]

These verses don't line up with Michel Onfray's point of view, or the views of other atheists as well. Baron d'Holbach went so far as to announce that Jesus forbids marriage!

> He [God's Son] teaches that, to attain to perfection, it is necessary to avoid marriage, and resist the strongest desire with which the breast of man is inspired—that of perpetuating his existence by a posterity and providing supports for his old age and infirmities.[9]

One has to wonder where these ideas came from. In any case, we can be certain that none of them came from the teachings of Jesus. I was relieved to discover that Christianity has nothing against sex, as long as it is enjoyed within the bounds of marriage. On the contrary, Christians who know their Bible can say a hearty *amen* to Baron d'Holbach when he declares: "It is not by extinguishing the passions of man that he is to be rendered happier; it is by turning them into proper channels, by directing them towards useful objects, which by being truly advantageous to himself, must of necessity be beneficial to others."[10]

I was over one hurdle, but the problem of abstinence before marriage remained. And there was no getting around it—Christianity indeed requires abstinence of believers until their wedding day.

This topic was a major minefield for me, but Robert crossed it brilliantly. Despite the obvious fact that I had broken this commandment and was openly hostile toward it, he wasn't defensive, critical, or judgmental. At the same time, he didn't compromise his point of view; he defended it intellectually and coherently.

Although I had a fair amount of animosity toward his ideas, I had to admit they made sense if God existed. If God exists, sex and marriage are part of his designed plan for humanity. And if God is the Creator, he has every right to regulate how our sexuality is expressed. If he created sex in the first place, he logically would be the one who would know the ideal conditions for its practice. On the other hand, if God *doesn't* exist, then marriage is merely a human invention and we should be free to do whatever we want as far as sexual relations go, before and after marriage.

The idea of some restrictions on sexuality didn't really bother me in itself. I think most people would agree that we should remain faithful to the person with whom we are in a relationship—though I hadn't always done so myself. God aside, most people in a committed relationship would not be comfortable sleeping with someone else or agreeing that their partner do the same—which is a sexual restriction of sorts.

But why is this important to us? For the same reason that Christianity forbids sex outside of marriage: because sex involves a powerful and special type of intimacy, which is best reserved for an exclusive and unconditional loving relationship.

Up to that point, I had cheated on every girl I had ever slept with, but even I would've had to admit that this was morally wrong and a failure on my part. To deny any sexual restrictions at all would mean accepting total sexual promiscuity, and even I wasn't that far gone.

André Comte-Sponville tells us that "there is no need for morals to intervene in sexual behavior between consenting adults."[11] I doubt he really believes that. If it were true, there would be no moral question about sexual vagrancy, orgies, adultery, incest between consenting adults, masochism, and prostitution (where both parties are consenting, as long as the price is right).

When Michel Onfray criticizes the sexual ethics of Christianity, he complains about "family, marriage, monogamy, fidelity," calling them all "variations on the theme of castration."[12] It is simply bewildering: If I don't want to be called a "castrator," or a moralist killjoy, must I deconstruct the family and engage in all sorts of sexual promiscuity, polygamy, and adultery? I'll pass, thank you. My own adventures in the world of sexual liberation convinced me of at least one thing: It's not the right path for me. I became disgusted with the cheating, the furious conquests, and the lies and the betrayals that ensued. In this area, I agreed that some adjustment to my behavior was probably not a bad idea. Despite my opposition to the concept of abstinence before marriage, as Robert and I talked, the idea of a more conservative view of sexuality began to seem more positive.

But was it humanly possible to be in a relationship and yet wait until marriage before sleeping together? Here again, Robert showed me that not only was it possible to wait, but it was also possible to hold a more traditional view of sexuality without losing one's mind. His own story served as a strong illustration of this.

Robert's wife, Kathryn, was the talented pianist and vocalist I had noticed in the church band during my first visit. Robert told me he hadn't even *kissed* her before they were married. Incredible! I told myself they were absolutely crazy—and anyway, it was too late for Vanessa and me to draw the line at kissing. Still, I found there was something powerful in the idea of saving the first kiss for the moment when the officiant says, "You may kiss the bride."

Even as I began to reconsider my approach to sexual ethics, I had yet another obstacle to get past—namely, why was it a problem for a Christian to marry a non-Christian?

Here again, some simple reflection was enough to help me understand that it wasn't a question of intolerance. Robert confirmed that the Bible instructs believers to marry "only in the Lord,"[13] and he calmly explained the verse in the Bible that mentions this. In short, it is a wise and practical standard when one considers that marriage (at least from a Christian point of view) is the most important human relationship we'll have in life.

Because (ideally) we commit ourselves for life to physical, intellectual, emotional, and sexual intimacy with one person, two people who enter this committed relationship must be on the same page. Of course, every couple has differing opinions on certain subjects, but having opposite viewpoints on God is not the same as one spouse pushing the toothpaste up from the bottom and the other from the top. What one believes about God's existence is one of the most fundamental issues of life.

Faith in God changes one's life completely, Robert explained, starting with the question "What is the goal of this earthly life?" Becoming a Christian would mean putting Jesus in the *center* of my existence. My wife's religious beliefs would affect all the big decisions we would make together. If I rolled my eyes every time she brought God into a discussion, our marriage wouldn't last very long. The conclusion seemed obvious to me: True intimacy with my wife would be impossible if I didn't share her deepest beliefs; and even more so if I found them ridiculous.

As a result of my research, I was beginning to realize that believing in Jesus would change my entire life. This might seem obvious, but I had never thought about it. I was also beginning to understand that my beliefs and my life projects would have to change if I wanted to become a Christian.

In order to keep my thoughts straight on the subject, I drew two columns on a sheet of paper, listing the pros and cons—the advantages and disadvantages—of becoming a Christian. Being able to marry Vanessa was definitely on the plus side, but abstinence before marriage was unquestionably a negative.

But once again, I quickly concluded that all these reasons had to be kept firmly outside of my final decision. I wouldn't become a Christian or remain an atheist because of how comfortable I felt or because of personal desire. I would decide based on my need to know the truth, and the truth had nothing to do with what I liked or disliked. *The truth of the matter*, I told myself, *should be based on a foundation of proof, reason, and science.*

Hostile science?

I was convinced that I had good scientific reasons to remain an atheist. Michel Onfray backed me up in saying that science and religion have always been at war with each other: "In science the church has always been wrong about everything: faced with an epistemological truth, it automatically persecutes the discoverer."[14] He mentions Galileo as an "emblematic representative of the church's hatred for science and of the conflict between faith and reason."[15] Moreover, Baron d'Holbach declared that "science must ever be at enmity with this religion; for in proportion as either of them gains ground the other must lose."[16] How could I legitimately switch sides in this intellectual battle? Ernest Renan argues that "it is not from one argument only but from the whole of modern science that the tremendous result is derived. 'There is no such thing as the supernatural.'"[17]

I had always believed that if truth was found in science, then faith could not affirm the opposite without committing intellectual suicide. If the existence of God flew in the face of a scientific theory, they could not both be true at the same time and in the same sense. Was this accurate? Were there scientific reasons why I should reject the idea of the existence of God? Or could science even confirm his existence? I realized that I needed to seriously consider these questions.

This was a crucial step in my reflection because it allowed me to realize, for the first time, that my atheism was not the result of a long and deep thought process, supported by advanced scholarly scientific proof that caused me to honestly question religion. It was, rather, a logical presupposition I held dear because all the intelligent people I had always been around seemed to be atheists. In my circle of friends and family, the question of God's existence had never been broached because we wouldn't have considered it worth our time. But now, when I gave it some serious thought, I had to admit that none of my scientific studies in high school or at the university where I earned my engineering degree were hostile to God's existence (or even pertinent to the subject). The only thing I could think of that even vaguely dealt with the possibility of God's existence was what I had been taught about the Big Bang and evolution—two theories I had studied in high school and in my prep classes for college. But in those classes, I had not come to any clear conclusions about the existence or nonexistence of God.

Later, I would discover some scientific reasons to support the idea that God does, indeed, exist. But for the time being, I concluded that I at least had no solid scientific reason to think he *didn't* exist.

Circular reasoning, naturalism, and materialism

In my studies of physics, I learned how the universe functions as long as it follows the laws of nature. But science doesn't establish that the world must *necessarily* follow the laws of nature, excluding any kind of supernatural intervention, or that nothing exists outside of nature. On the contrary, this theory, called naturalism, is a *philosophical presupposition*, not a scientific conclusion. It is certainly a *widely accepted* presupposition, but it's a presupposition nonetheless. Baron d'Holbach based his writing of *The System of Nature* on the assumption that nothing exists outside of the natural world, and he declares it as a creed at the very beginning of that voluminous work:

> Man is the work of Nature; he exists in Nature; he is submitted to her laws: he cannot deliver himself from them. . . . The beings which he pictures to himself as above nature, or distinguished from her, are always chimeras formed after that which he has

already seen, but of which it is impossible he should ever form any correct idea, either as to the place they occupy, or of their manner of acting. There is not, there can be nothing out of that Nature which includes all beings.[18]

If this is true, then of course God cannot exist. But if naturalism is our starting point, then the atheist's conclusion is not very interesting. It is an example of circular reasoning, barely more sophisticated than saying, "God doesn't exist because God doesn't exist."

We find the same problem in another, similar theory called *materialism*. This theory claims that *matter* is the only thing that truly exists. And here again, if materialism is true, then God cannot exist because God is not material. However, we cannot *presuppose* this theory to disprove the existence of God.

Jean Meslier, an eighteenth-century priest and closet atheist, said in a statement published after his death, "It is obvious that the material being is in all things, that all things are made of material being, which is to say, from matter itself."[19]

At the risk of sounding foolish, I don't see how this theory is at all "obvious," and Meslier didn't tell us. His circular reasoning is underlined by this illuminating summary by commentator Serge Deruette: "Meslier, affirming and reaffirming that everything is matter and that matter is everything, approaches the subject as a materialist, and concludes it as an atheist."[20] No kidding! Meslier's starting point determines his conclusion.

Michel Onfray gives us his own version of this circular

reasoning when he states that "the existence of these atoms explained the makeup of all matter, and consequently of the world itself."[21] The word *consequently* is unjustified in this sentence: Onfray presupposes that matter is the only thing that truly exists in our world.[22] Then he adds that "materialism has been the fly in Christianity's ointment from the beginning. The church stops at nothing to discredit this coherent philosophy and its complete account of all reality."[23] Once again, the supposed capacity of materialism to explain absolutely everything real is a gratuitous statement. Materialism is apparently a "coherent philosophy" for Onfray. But *coherence does not entail truth*. As a simple example, consider these two statements: "I am an American adult" and "I have the right to vote." They are coherent, and both are *false* in my case. I am a French citizen and do not have the right to vote in the United States.

Finally, Onfray issues one last accusation in the section of his chapter on materialism, subheaded "Negation of matter." He confuses the rejection of materialism with the negation of matter. He correctly understands that belief in the existence of God demands a rejection of materialism: "And of course, if everything is made up of matter, soul, spirit, and gods as well share that makeup."[24] But he adds a ludicrous statement describing monotheisms as having "a strong aversion to matter and reality, therefore all forms of immanence."[25] Ridiculous! Of course, believers affirm the existence of matter; they simply also believe that *something else* exists. This in no way implies a "hatred of matter," despite Onfray's dogged assertions.[26]

As I contemplated these lines of reasoning, I saw that none supported the accusation that science refutes theism. Thus, I tentatively concluded that the question was still open. Science doesn't tell us *too much* to allow for a belief in God. But maybe it isn't telling us *enough*. Is it perhaps necessary to prove the existence of God scientifically in order to believe?

Scientism

Toward the end of my studies in the mathematics prep class I took before entering my engineering studies, my math teacher ended one of our class sessions with an unexpected and solemn warning. He said something like this:

> Ladies and gentlemen, you are now officially experts
> in math, physics, and engineering science. You have
> spent the past few years mastering vector spaces,
> multivariate functions, differential equations,
> Newton's laws, the mechanics of solids and fluids,
> thermodynamics, electromagnetism, and many other
> complex subjects. You are, therefore, considered to
> be specialists in several important fields of science.
> It would only be natural, then, for you to think that
> you have become *more intelligent* and knowledgeable
> in *more important* areas of study than your friends

who are seeking degrees in literature, sociology, or history, right?

Obviously, I thought to myself.
"Well, you are absolutely wrong!"
What an unexpected wake-up call! The teacher had perfectly anticipated my scientific arrogance, and he spent the next few minutes passionately criticizing it.

These other fields of intellectual exploration are *just as important* and necessary to society. Your scientific knowledge is extremely important, but I beg of you, don't fall for the idea that what you have learned is more important or impressive than what others are doing in their respective professions. Science is not all there is to life!

This warning, uttered by a foremost specialist in the queen of all sciences, my brilliant math teacher, made such an impression on me that I still remember it clearly, more than twenty years later. At the time, I concluded that he was probably right. But the idea he exposed was so deeply ingrained in me that, despite his warning, as I contemplated the existence of God, I still had to answer a crucial question: Shouldn't I believe exclusively in what science tells me? This theory, sometimes called *scientism*, avows that science should be our only trustworthy source of knowledge. It was mostly popular in the nineteenth century, but we still find adherents today, especially among atheist scientists. Philosopher Jacques Bouveresse (himself an atheist) actually *denounced* this theory in the writings of Sigmund Freud and Bertrand Russell:

> In the last sentence of *The Future of an Illusion*, Freud states that science is not an illusion (as religion is): "No, our science is no illusion. But an illusion it would be to suppose that what science cannot give us we can get elsewhere."
>
> We are obviously much more willing today to admit that there are, even in matters of so-called knowledge, other sources from which we can hope to receive what science cannot give us. In other words, we would be hard-pressed to find many people who would proclaim Russell as being right when he says that "whatever knowledge is attainable, must be attained by scientific methods; and what science cannot discover, mankind cannot know."[27]

I wish I shared Bouveresse's optimism when he says it would be difficult to find many people who believe in the thesis of scientism today. It may be nearly nonexistent in academic circles, but sadly I fear it is still widespread among the general public. Proponents of scientism are often atheists, sometimes scientists, whose reasoning goes something like this: "Science is our only reliable source of knowledge, and the existence of God is not a scientific theory; therefore, it is not reasonable to believe that God exists."

Christians are free to try to refute this argument by showing that science actually supports the existence of God. But it may be more effective (and easier) to simply refute the presupposition of scientism, which frankly doesn't have a leg to stand on. Science is not in any way our only reliable source of knowledge, and there are many counterexamples that prove this to be true.

- The laws of logic are not scientifically established; on the contrary, they are presupposed. Yet we know they are true and essential to any intellectual discipline, including science.

- Metaphysical truths are things we know to be true outside of scientific methods. For example, the outside world truly exists, and I am not merely a brain in a vat being manipulated by a mad scientist who wants to make me believe in the outside world. Or, the past is real; the world was not created five minutes ago with apparent age.

- Ethics is another area of nonscientific but fully rational knowledge: Science can tell us that giving poison to a *Homo sapiens* will kill him or her, but it cannot show us, using the scientific method, that murder is wrong.

- Aesthetics (the philosophy of art) is another example. I know that a sunset or a Monet painting is beautiful, but science doesn't tell me that. Science can only tell me why the sunset is comprised of certain colors and how the paint stays on the canvas, but it does not establish that these things are beautiful—or even what beauty is.

I could add other more or less convincing counter-examples, and if even *one* of these counterexamples is true, then scientism is false. But it gets worse: We can deal the final blow by simply stating that scientism *refutes itself*. Indeed, the claim that science is our only source of reasonable knowledge is itself not a scientifically supported thesis. If scientism is true, by its own affirmation we cannot affirm it! This is a fatal flaw and it clearly explains why scientism is in such decline today.

I was thus forced to accept that it is possible for us to know things, even if they aren't scientific.

As I continued meeting with Robert and thinking about what I was discovering, all of my initial intellectual barriers began to crumble. I accepted the fact that it was possible to be intelligent and still believe in the supernatural. I understood that the Christian view of marriage wasn't as old-fashioned or intolerant as I once believed it to be. I concluded that science didn't say too much or too little for me to believe in the assertions of Christianity that God exists and that Jesus rose from the dead. But if I were to affirm such theories, I would need some good supporting reasons. I needed to *know*.

There is no room for doubt, I told myself. *If I'm going to change my mind about Christianity, I need to be absolutely certain.*

7

Searching for Certainty

• • •

*If you meet someone who tells you: "I know
that God exists," he is an idiot who has
faith and takes it to be knowledge.*

ANDRÉ COMTE-SPONVILLE

BEFORE I COULD ACCEPT Christianity intellectually, I knew I
would have to accept the existence of God and the miracles
of Jesus, especially his resurrection. But how could I be sure
about those things? The stakes were high, and I wanted to
be absolutely certain. I didn't want to make a rash decision
to become a Christian and wind up looking like an idiot
when confronted with irrefutable counterarguments. As I
spent time discussing various issues with Robert and continued my own research, I began to consider the *truthfulness* of
Christianity. From there, I naturally began seeking certainty
about what I was discovering.

Certainty. Is it a reasonable expectation? It is undoubtedly a widespread and common assumption that before we can say we *know* something, especially as far as religion is concerned, we must be able to *prove* it. André Comte-Sponville, for example, raises the question of the existence of God. But before weighing the arguments, he states, "No science, it should be repeated, can answer this question—nor can any form of knowledge."[1]

On the plus side, Comte-Sponville's statement shows that (unlike scientism, as we've seen) he believes there may be knowledge outside of science. But why would he believe it's impossible to know whether God exists? Comte-Sponville says that anyone who "knows" something must be able to justify it so strongly as to convince anyone:

> On the subject of God's existence, what intelligent
> and lucid person could claim to have knowledge;
> that is, a subjectively *and objectively* sufficient
> credence? If such a thing was possible, then that
> person should be able to convince us, for it is in
> the nature of knowledge to be transmittable to any
> normally intelligent and cultivated individual, and
> atheism would long ago have vanished.[2]

This is not a realistic standard, and it flies in the face of so many counterexamples. Imagine that I'm being set up for a crime I did not commit. Since all the evidence points to my guilt, I could probably never convince a jury made up of "normally intelligent and cultivated individuals" of my innocence. However, that doesn't prevent me from *knowing* I am innocent. This very simple example directly refutes Comte-Sponville's statement.

Even without imagining such an outlandish situation, we can agree that knowledge doesn't require the elimination of all dissent. Given the prevalence of human bias and prejudice, especially ideological biases, this would be impossible anyway, even in the mind of "any normally intelligent and cultivated individual." Conspiracy theorists, misled zealots, and people who deny that the Holocaust happened may be "intelligent and cultivated," but they are nonetheless extremely prejudiced. Their intelligence and urbanity don't prevent us from *knowing* (not just thinking) they are wrong.

Jean Meslier demands this same type of proof concerning Jesus' miracles:

> We cannot be certain that any of these miracles
> actually took place, just as we cannot be certain of
> the trustworthiness or the sincerity of those who
> reported the miracles or claimed to be eyewitnesses.
> There is no way to confirm that they were familiar
> with or even took note of the circumstances, nor that
> the stories we read were even written by those who
> claimed to write them. And finally, there is no way
> to be sure that these stories were not corrupted and
> falsified as we know so many others to have been.[3]

In some ways, I think most Christians would agree. There are no absolute and undeniable *certainties* concerning these subjects. But why do we need this type of assurance to *know* that the teachings of Christianity are true? "Absolute certainty" is a very poor standard of knowledge. In fact, as I will explain in a moment, it's downright irrational. Nonetheless, Jean Meslier bases his argument on this exaggerated requirement. He proceeds to add another layer to his illogical reasoning when he states that if Christians cannot prove their theories with certainty, Christianity itself is refuted:

> If none of those who proclaim their religion to be of divine institution can give proof and sure and convincing testimony, this is clear and convincing proof that none of these religions are truly divine. Therefore, we must hold as evident that they are all of human invention and filled with errors, illusions, and trickery.[4]

No. Meslier's line of reasoning is completely invalid. Absence of proof is not proof of absence. Ask any police officer—or anyone who has ever played the game Clue. Just because I cannot prove that Colonel Mustard killed Mr. Boddy with the candlestick in the billiard room doesn't mean he is *not* the murderer. In the absence of proof, one should at most refrain from offering an opinion.

And that's not all. We often *know* things without being absolutely certain about them or without being able to prove them beyond a shadow of a doubt. Theories that insist that "knowledge requires proof" or "knowledge requires certainty" are faulty on two fronts:

1. They tend to refute themselves.
2. They fall victim to numerous counterexamples.

A standard that contradicts itself

Unrealistically expecting *proof* or *certainty* tends to lead one down the same path that scientism did—by formulating demands that are self-defeating. Scientism clearly falls into this category when it insists that we must not believe (or cannot know) anything but science. Unfortunately, this theory itself does not derive from science.

And we run into the same problem with the claim that we cannot know anything without being able to prove it: We're unable to prove the claim! The same is true of certainty: No one can be certain of the theory that says we must be certain. In other words, it is not irrefutable that knowledge must be irrefutable. All these requirements refute themselves.

Accordingly, many atheist thinkers who try to make demands concerning God and his existence often make self-refuting statements. In Jacques Monod's opinion, "The systematic confronting of logic and experience is the sole source of true knowledge."[5] Except that the knowledge of his claim is in no way obtained by confronting logic and experience. What confrontation of "logic and experience" could Monod have conducted that would lead to this conclusion? I can't think of any.

Baron d'Holbach gives us his version: "From the constant relation which is made by well-constituted senses, results that evidence and that certitude which can alone produce full conviction."[6] But this is not a belief that results from the use of the baron's five well-constituted senses. Neither evidence nor certitude results from this, and he should, therefore, not be fully convinced.

Believing, and even knowing, without proof or certainty

The logical and theoretical problem of being self-refuting is insurmountable, and I actually find it quite amusing, but let's get back to the practical side of things. What are some things in our day-to-day lives that we believe, and even *know* rationally, but cannot prove beyond a shadow of a doubt? Some of the things we discussed in the previous chapter as counterexamples for scientism would be found on this list: the laws of logic, metaphysics, ethics, and beauty, to name a few. We know all these things without proof or absolute certainty.

For example, it's impossible to *prove* the laws of logic because any argument in their favor would have to be based on the laws of logic. We would have to presuppose that the laws of logic are true in order to prove them, which is fallacious, circular reasoning.

The existence of the outside world and the reality of the past are also impossible to prove. We cannot claim to have any absolute certainty about them. I cannot remove myself from my five senses to verify that my perception of the outside world is veridical. Nevertheless, it is clearly rational for me to believe that the outside world really does exist. I *know* that the outside world is real, despite the lack of proof or absolute certainty. In the same way, I cannot prove the validity of my memories of the past, but I know they are real.

Now I'd like to add some additional, obvious counterexamples to this list. These items became very relevant to me as I spent time talking to Robert and examining Christianity.

I know, without any proof or absolute certainty, my name. I know who my father is. I know my birth date and the name of the hospital where I was born. I know that July 14 is Bastille Day in France, even though I can never remember the year it happened. And I know that Caesar crossed the Rubicon in 49 BC. I know that the Great Wall of China exists. I've never seen it for myself, but I'm as sure of its existence as I am of the Empire State Building, which I see out my window every morning. I know who the French president is, I know that Mont Blanc is 4,807 meters high,[7] and I know it rains a lot in Seattle.

I know all these things, without proof and without absolute certainty. How? Because in each case, *someone who knows told me it was true.*

Yes, personal testimonies are a valid source of knowledge, a source of *knowing*, not just of believing.

Blind faith or eyewitness testimonies?

I was sitting on the sofa in Robert's office one evening, and we were having one of our many discussions about religion. I immediately captured his attention when I said, "Robert, I've been thinking about it, and I don't think it's reasonable for me to demand absolute certainty concerning Christianity."

He sat up in his chair. He looked intrigued.

"Well," I continued, "what I don't want to do is believe stories about Jesus based on *blind faith*. I want to have some good reasons to believe. I want my beliefs to be *warranted*. I want to *know* that these events really took place. When I think about it, there are a lot of things that I *know* without having any iron-clad proof. I know they are true because someone trustworthy told me they were true. As I've been reading the Bible these past few months, I've realized that the Gospels are exactly that: a collection of *personal testimonies*. It's like having four friends who are telling me about something that happened when I wasn't there. The texts of Matthew, Mark, Luke, and John all tell the same basic story. If their testimonies are trustworthy, I can know that these things really happened, even though I wasn't there at the time. When you think about it, it's a bit like having a friend today tell me about something that happened. If I believe my friend when he tells me something that way, why wouldn't I believe it when it's four of them?"

For once, Robert didn't have much to add. He realized this was an important moment of understanding for me. He just smiled.

Historical criticism of the Gospels

Now, someone who reads this will no doubt respond that it's not that simple. We don't want to be so gullible as to believe everything people tell us. I agree. Absolutely. That's why we must add the proviso that a person's testimony provides knowledge only if that testimony is *trustworthy*.

So what about the Gospel accounts? Can they be trusted? Do they allow us to know the truth about Jesus?

The four Gospels have been routinely criticized, and their historical reliability has been debated by scholars, critics, and commentators. To begin with, skeptical critics sometimes complain that the four Gospels that made it into the New Testament were chosen arbitrarily, while other documents (such as the so-called Infancy gospel of Thomas, the gospel of Barnabas, the gospel of Peter, the gospel of Judas, and others) are considered apocryphal books and thus were rejected.

The French religious historian Prosper Alfaric says that "nothing in the light of pure criticism justifies this favoritism,"[8] but he is wrong—this so-called favoritism is absolutely justified. The canonical Gospels are attributed to eyewitnesses or direct disciples of Jesus, and we are able to verify today that they reflect an awareness of the names of Palestinian Jews of the first century.[9] They also demonstrate familiarity with the geography of the region, including its vegetation.[10] The apocryphal books, on the other hand, were written later by men who were not direct associates of Jesus and lack any specific or verifiable information on people or places involved in Jesus' life.[11] Many of these texts reflect the teaching of a later sect called the Gnostics, who appeared in the second century of the common era. The Gnostics were obviously far removed from Jesus' Palestinian Jewish disciples.

Even Ernest Renan, who was not a great fan of Christianity, insisted that the apocryphal writings were "insipid and puerile amplifications, having the Canonical Gospels for their basis, and adding nothing thereto of any value."[12]

The early dates attributed to the writing of the Gospels also count in favor of their reliability: Conservative estimates date them between AD 50 and 90, and even the most liberal estimates place them between AD 70 and 120. Even if the later dates are correct, these documents were written remarkably close to the time of the events they describe.

French geneticist and essayist Albert Jacquard denounced these dates as being too late for the Gospels to be reliable.[13] But if that's true, we must shut down every department of ancient history in all our universities. If historical documents written within 120 years are not sufficient, we're left with precious little evidence for anything that happened in the distant past. Take, for example, the exploits of Alexander the Great. Nobody entertains wholesale doubts about their veracity. But the best available sources were all written hundreds of years after Alexander's death. (Apparently, several of his peers wrote about him, but their writings have been lost to history.[14]) Among the remaining texts are those written by Diodorus, Strabo, Quintus Curtius, Arrian, and Plutarch, the earliest of which was written some three hundred years after Alexander's death. The latter two, which are also the most reliable, date to between 425 and 450 years after his death.[15] The Gospels (and Paul's letters) are much closer to the events *they* describe.

The identities of the authors of the Gospels have also been criticized. Prosper Alfaric says, "We don't even know their real names, because the names Matthew, Mark, Luke, and John cannot be guaranteed and seem to be fictitious."[16]

Once again, his criticism is unwarranted. Naturally, we cannot *guarantee* the identities of the biblical authors. Who could impose such an unrealistic standard on any ancient historical document? Nevertheless, our most reliable extra-biblical historical sources, those whose dates are closest to the events, identify the authors as Matthew, Mark, Luke and John.[17] No alternative theory is offered in ancient writings that would suggest a different authorship.

Another indicator of historical reliability—multiplicity of sources—should also be noted. If several independent sources report the same event, it is unlikely the authors all agreed to tell the same lie. Here again, the Christian sources are very well positioned. Paul's letters include some ancient creeds; John's Gospel with its unique content, and the other three, more similar Gospels (often called the synoptic Gospels), give us abundant information about the life of Jesus. Prosper Alfaric denied the multiplicity of sources, dismissing the three synoptic Gospels as "resembling a chain which hangs from the first link."[18] But this is an incorrect view of the biblical sources. The standard model, agreed upon by the majority of biblical scholars (including atheists), maintains that there are no less than four or five independent sources behind the synoptic Gospels.[19] Add to these Paul's letters and we have an incredible abundance of multiple historical sources, unmatched when dealing with a historical figure who dates as far back as Jesus does.

But can we trust the documents we have today, knowing that they are not the originals, written by the original authors, but are imperfect, handwritten copies? When we inspect and compare the copies of the New Testament documents we have today, we find numerous textual variations. In fact, many thousands of differences have been noted. Jean Meslier takes the Bible to task on this matter, claiming that the documents we rely on are filled with "subtractions and falsifications."[20]

Is this an accurate representation of the facts? No. There are indeed many subtractions among the manuscripts, and also many additions, different word arrangements, and substitutions. But *falsifications*? That's a stretch. The vast majority of variations are simple differences in spelling or word order and have no effect on the meaning of the text itself. A large proportion of variants are found in lone manuscripts or very late manuscripts, and have no credibility.

As to the passages where there seem to be some differences in meaning, we must compare manuscripts to see which ones are closer to the original text. In the vast majority of cases in the New Testament, we can identify without much difficulty the variations that almost certainly do not carry the original words. Indeed, in order to reconstruct the full original text of a historical document for which we only have copies—and often only fragments of documents—we need *many* copies, and we need them to be *old*.

As it happens, the New Testament is far superior to any other Greco-Roman literature in this regard. Today, we have more than 5,500 manuscripts in Greek, approximately 10,000 in Latin, and thousands more in other languages. As far as age, the oldest papyrus fragment from the New Testament is called P52 and has been dated to AD 100–150—just a few dozen years at most after the original was written. The first nearly complete copies of single New Testament books appeared around AD 200, and the earliest complete copy of the New Testament, the Codex Sinaiticus, dates to the fourth century. Today, there are nearly one thousand extant manuscripts of the New Testament in Greek dating to AD 1000 or earlier. And, of course, many more in ancient translations.

Compare this to the works of Plato, Caesar, or Tacitus, from whom we have only a few hundred copies, with the earliest sometimes dating as late as one thousand years after the original writings. Scholars of Greco-Roman authors complain about a dearth of data, while noting that New Testament scholars have an embarrassment of riches. If we doubt that our Bible manuscripts go back to the originals, then our doubts about the average ancient Greek or Latin author's original words would be *a thousand times greater*.

In a nutshell, the New Testament is in a category of its own, far above any competition, and so much so that the textual variations don't give us any reason to doubt the reliability of the sources.[21]

I am summarizing these arguments here because it is helpful to answer this important question that was naturally raised by my story, but during the months when I was meeting with Robert, I hadn't yet studied most of the best Bible critics or their arguments. Therefore, I wasn't in any position to try to disprove what they were saying. Could I, nonetheless, trust the Gospels and know that what they were telling me about Jesus was true? I maintain that I could. Why is that? It is because someone who reads a trustworthy historical account can actually know that its content is true, without ever researching the opposing critical arguments. Consider an example: I know that the Holocaust happened during the Second World War, and I have known it since elementary school. I now also know that there are people who want to deny that it ever occurred. I don't know what their arguments are, but I'm sure they have some. Since I don't know what those arguments are, I am unable to disprove them, but my lack of knowledge on the subject doesn't prevent me from knowing that the Holocaust occurred. This is due to the strength of the testimonies I've heard, which carry much more authority than the objectors' arguments.

Christians affirm something quite similar when it comes to God's existence and the truth of the biblical documents. It is possible to read the historical texts and come to the conclusion that Jesus died and also rose from the dead, based on trustworthy historical testimonies, without ever reading, much less disproving, the critiques I addressed above.

But now, if the Gospels are historically trustworthy, why are so many people skeptical of their content? I believe it is largely because they report on Jesus' miracles. Their historical skepticism tends to be in proportion to their closed-mindedness concerning miracles. But it was this same closed-minded refusal to even consider the possibility of supernatural occurrences that was slowly but surely dissipating as I continued my conversations with Robert. Gradually, I was able to set aside my absurd expectation of "absolute certainty" and abandon my insistence that miracles were impossible in principle. As I honestly read the Gospels and my mind became more open to what I was reading, I could finally ask myself the question: *Could all of this be true?*

Miracles: History or Mythology?

• • •

*Christian faith had nothing to gain (and rather
more to lose) by tying its fate to supernatural events
whose credibility becomes more fragile every day.*

LUC FERRY

ON ANOTHER ONE OF MY VISITS with Robert at Le Bon Berger
(The Good Shepherd), the church he and his wife had established in Paris, I said to him, "Tell me about miracles, Robert.
I'm a little more open now to the idea of miracles when I read
about them in the Bible. I'm no longer opposed *in principle*
to the possibility. But I'm just not sure what to think. I don't
want to be too skeptical *or* too naïve. Have you seen any miracles? What is your personal experience in this area?"

"That's a great question," Robert replied. "For Christians,
the most important miracles are those performed by Jesus.
But yes, I can also tell you some personal stories.

"Here's one that really touched me.

"When my second daughter, Réanna, was born, we prayed and sang around her bed. We felt the Lord was telling us that she would somehow take a message of healing to the world. No one but God knew that our baby girl was very sick at the time.

"Several days after we brought her home from the hospital, she became very pale. She wouldn't eat and her body was almost lifeless. On Saturday evening, we realized how ill she really was. We prayed all night, but she didn't improve. At church on Sunday morning, we felt as if God was telling us that he was going to heal our baby. Kathryn took Réanna to the hospital while I stayed to preach.

"While the doctors were running some tests on Réanna's heart, Kathryn looked down and yelled, 'She's not breathing!' A doctor who happened to be passing in the hall grabbed Réanna and ran with her in his arms to the emergency room, where they tried to bring her back for more than twenty minutes.

"When I got to the hospital, the doctor came out of the emergency room with some terrible news: 'Your baby has a blocked aorta, several holes in her ventricles, renal failure, liver failure, and serious cerebral anomalies that indicate irreversible damage. She won't survive the night; and if she does, she'll be in a vegetative state the rest of her life.'

"We asked the members of our church to pray, and Réanna's situation soon became known around the world. Christians as far away as New Zealand were praying for her. The doctors decided to operate on her heart to open her aorta, but they said the rest was up to Réanna.

"'No, the rest is up to God,' I told them.

"Three weeks later, Réanna was in perfect health. The holes in her heart had closed up, her liver and kidneys began working, and the brain lesions disappeared. When she was six years old, I took her back for some tests to verify that her aorta was growing correctly. One of the doctors remembered her. He told me: 'You know, what happened to Réanna, we don't see that every day around here.' After an ultrasound, he said, 'It's incredible, but you can't even tell that her aorta has been operated on, much less that it was once blocked.' I asked him to write that in a letter, which I've kept to this day."

"Hmmm . . . yeah, that's quite remarkable," I said, after a moment of silence. "What a story! And didn't you tell me that you had a sort of 'vision' the day you became a Christian? Can you tell me more about that?"

"I was fourteen years old when a cute girl from my science class invited me to a movie. It was being shown by the Bible club at school. I couldn't have cared less about the Bible, but I wanted to go out with the girl, so I went. And then the cute girl never showed up! But instead of leaving, I felt that I should stay and watch the movie. So I walked into the room and sat down.

"The film was about the last days and the Lord's second coming. At the end of the movie, I didn't know why, but I started crying and couldn't stop. Someone turned on the lights, and I buried my face in my hands to hide my tears. In desperation, I prayed, 'My God, turn out the lights.' All of a sudden, the lights went out again, and another film started.

"This one was about a young pregnant lady arriving at a hospital. She looked a lot like my own mom at the same age. And suddenly I knew (somehow) that I was the baby about to be born. I didn't understand how it was possible, but I was watching a film about my own life. Each time I committed a sin, the film would stop, and I would feel more and more guilty. By the end of the movie, I was completely shaken and crying uncontrollably. Behind the screen, I saw a great throne, but I couldn't see the face of the person seated on it. I saw a large hand, and its index finger was pointing straight at me. A loud voice declared, 'Guilty!' In despair, I saw myself dragged away from the throne, and I felt the temperature rising until my back felt like it was burning. I heard voices screaming in agony in this hellish scene . . .

"And then the lights came back on and I was back in the classroom, surrounded by the other students. A young man took the microphone and said, 'If you have any questions about what you just saw and heard, we have counselors ready to talk and pray with you.' I ran to the front of the class, and that day, I met Jesus Christ. He took over my life, and I've never looked back."

I found Robert's stories interesting, though they were purely anecdotal. But I remembered the strange experience I'd had myself coming out of his church after my first visit.

But it wasn't irrefutable, I told myself. There could easily have been a natural explanation for the shivers I'd felt when going out the door that day.

The healing of Robert's daughter was pretty exceptional, but I knew things like that happened sometimes. As far as Robert's vision went, dreams or even hallucinations aren't that rare. In short, nothing from these stories was really conclusive—though I had to admit that the circumstances were quite interesting. Still, I found I agreed with Robert that the most essential miracles were the ones performed by Jesus and recorded by trustworthy historical sources. My skepticism toward them was mostly fueled by the naturalistic presuppositions I held.

Naturalistic presuppositions against miracles

Atheistic thinkers typically are not fond of miracles. Which isn't all that surprising. After all, a miracle requires divine intervention. If there is no God, there are no miracles. No problem there: We can't blame atheists for wanting to be consistent and reasonable.

The problem begins when they use atheism as a *starting point*—that is, when they evaluate and criticize the reliability of miraculous accounts in the Bible based on their atheistic presuppositions and convictions. If you exclude the very possibility that a miracle could happen before you even look at the evidence, what are the chances you'll recognize a miracle if you see one when you do evaluate the historical evidence?

Unfortunately, this type of preemptive reasoning is quite common in historical criticism of the New Testament. For example, Albert Jacquard, speaking of Christ's resurrection, says, "We are faced with an unprecedented affirmation, an impossible event. If death's irreversibility is negated, if this transformation of our being is no longer definitive, then the most reliable certainties waver."[1] Accordingly, he insists, the scientist "can only express his doubt, and even in the face of such implausible facts admit with near certainty that these events, as they were reported, could not have happened."[2]

Jacquard is utterly unable to set aside his atheism to consider a possibility beyond its bounds. Obviously, miracles are *naturally* impossible. But if there is an all-powerful God beyond nature, and he has a good reason for raising someone from the dead, then resurrection becomes possible *supernaturally*. It is not our "most reliable certainties" that waver; only our presupposition of atheism.

Baron d'Holbach is not much more open-minded when he says,

> As for those effects, which are called *miracles*, that is to say, contrary to the immutable laws of nature, such things are impossible; because nothing can for an instant suspend the necessary course of beings, without arresting the entire of nature, and disturbing her in her tendency.[3]

Baron d'Holbach is in such a hurry to declare the impossibility of miracles that he goes so far as to say that they would be impossible for God himself!

A miracle is a thing impossible in the order of
nature. If this be changed by God, he is not
immutable. . . . God himself, therefore, cannot
perform miracles without counteracting the
institutions of his own wisdom.[4]

It is difficult to understand the motivation behind his
affirmation, and thus equally difficult to criticize it, except
by saying there is simply no reason to believe it.

Ernest Renan claims to be open to the possibility of miracles and to not base his conclusions about them on his own
philosophical presuppositions.

It is not, then, in the name of this or that philosophy,
but in the name of unbroken experience, that we
banish the miracle from history. We do not say, "The
miracle is impossible." We say, "So far, a miracle has
never been proved."[5]

But after pleading *not guilty*, he immediately puts his foot
in his mouth and commits the very same mistake: affirming
that his historical interpretative methodology leaves no room
for accepting the miraculous.

Until the order of things changes, we maintain it,
then, as a principle of historical criticism, that a
supernatural account cannot be admitted as such,
that it always implies credulity or imposture, that it

is the duty of the historian to explain it, and search out what share of truth, or of error, it may conceal.[6]

Renan preemptively excludes any possible evidence of the miraculous—as a matter of principle—"until the order of things changes" (or, I suppose, until hell freezes over). If a miracle did happen, he would not admit it because his methodology already excluded it.

We find naturalistic presuppositions as well in the dating of the Gospels. Prosper Alfaric lays out this classic argument in favor of a later date:

> One thing is indisputable. The Gospels were written long after the times of which they speak. They were all written after 70 AD, since they all allude to the destruction of the Temple in Jerusalem which took place that year, during the war of the Jews.[7]

This is not at all undisputed, much less indisputable. When the Gospel writers alluded to the destruction of the Temple, they were recounting Jesus' *prophecy*, where he announced the destruction beforehand to warn his disciples.[8]

Obviously, if we presuppose naturalism, we must place the writing of the Gospels some time *after* the AD 70 events, to say that the authors were able to insert the destruction of the Temple into the narrative because they were familiar with the history of it. But for someone who is open to the possibility that Jesus would know the future, this is not a valid reason to date the Gospels after AD 70. Once again, we must reject circular reasoning here. It is clearly biased against the possibility of the supernatural. And Alfaric isn't afraid to admit it. In his reading of the Gospels, he presupposes that "miracle" equates with "mythology."

> They recount the strangest, most unbelievable stories imaginable. The blind see, the deaf hear, paralytics walk, demon-possessed people are freed from their chains, sick people are suddenly healed, the dying are revived, the dead are raised: such are the tales they tell. We are right in the midst of ancient mythology. . . .
> The more a story is filled with the extraordinary, the more we must beware of the "facts" purported, even the simplest and most natural among them. In such circumstances, methodical doubt must prevail.[9]

This "methodical doubt," based on Alfaric's naturalistic presuppositions, leaves no room for an impartial study of historical sources. Moreover, his "methodical doubt" leads him to a particularly radical position, one that has been revived in recent times, particularly in France, by Michel Onfray. Alfaric and Onfray do not stop with denying miracles; they go so far as to deny the existence of Jesus of Nazareth.

Who knows?

With enough skepticism, one can deny almost anything. I'm not saying such denial is reasonable, but it's obviously possible. So we can't be surprised when skeptics deny the existence of a historical Jesus. Bertrand Russell sets the tone here: "Historically, it is quite doubtful whether Christ ever existed at all, and if He did we do not know anything about Him."[10]

Michel Onfray proposes this theory: "Jesus's existence has not been historically established. No contemporary documentation of the event, no archaeological proof, nothing certain exists today to attest to the truth of a real presence."[11]

Once again, we see an unreasonable attempt at certainty, coupled with a radical skepticism about Jesus' existence. This theory is held by a small minority, even in atheistic circles, but because several popular partisans have a large media following, we must examine the question seriously (even if we might think it doesn't deserve to be taken seriously).

So why should we consider the negationist theory to be unreasonable? Quite simply, because Jesus' existence is supported by a *multitude* of *independent* historical sources, dating back to a time *close* to the actual events, and which are practically impossible to explain if Jesus didn't at least exist.

First, he is mentioned outside the Bible, in both Jewish and pagan sources, including: Flavius Josephus, Suetonius, and Tacitus. This is actually a surprising wealth of sources compared to what we might expect to find in ancient sources about a somewhat obscure Jew from a little town in Palestine.

For transparency's sake, we must note that Josephus's account is somewhat problematic because he affirms that Jesus is the Messiah. This is fairly improbable coming from a non-Christian Jew, as Josephus was. It is, therefore, commonly held that this clause is an interpolation; that is, a later addition to the text by Christian scribes.

Michel Onfray uses this point to justify a wholesale rejection of all this evidentiary material. He asserts that the writings of Josephus, Suetonius, and Tacitus "obey the rules of intellectual forgery," that later Christian scribes interpolated the text, inserting Jesus into these Jewish and Roman writings.[12]

This is much too fast. Specialists of Josephus's writing (mostly non-Christians) claim that the passage is not all interpolation and, at the very least, that Josephus is speaking of Jesus of Nazareth and of the events that surrounded him in Judea during the first century. As for Suetonius and Tacitus, there are no textual reasons (i.e., no variants found in alternate manuscripts) or contextual reasons (such as Josephus's unexpected claim of Christ's messiahship) to doubt the relevant passages. Thus, it is entirely unjustified to claim that their writings contain interpolations. Moreover, it is improbable that Christians would have inserted the phrases we are dealing with since they are fundamentally derogatory toward Jesus and his disciples. We may, therefore, consider these sources as valid.

Even Ernest Renan affirms their reliability: "Would it . . . be writing the history of Jesus to omit those sermons which exhibit to us in such a vivid manner the nature of his discourses, and to limit ourselves to saying, with Josephus and Tacitus, 'that he was put to death by the order of Pilate' at the instigation of the priests?"[13]

In any case, these are not the most pertinent historical sources concerning Jesus. They may serve as an interesting confirmation, but the main historical writings on Jesus' life are the four Gospels and Paul's epistles. So let's take a look at what the negationists have to say about them.

Parallelism and parallelomania

Skeptics such as Onfray and Alfaric affirm what are called *mythicist* theories, which hypothesize that the Gospels are invented stories inspired by pagan mythology. Michel Onfray suggests that Jesus "shares some similarities with Homer's Ulysses and with Encolpius, one of the protagonists in Petronius's *Satyricon*. The writer Philostratus wrote a biography of Apollonius of Tyana, which some have seen as an attempt to construct a rival to Jesus Christ. In other words, Jesus is an epic hero among other epic heroes."[14]

Even though Baron d'Holbach doesn't go so far as to deny Jesus' existence, he dismisses him as "a poor Jew, who pretended to be descended from the royal house of David" but who was "incapable of . . . convincing the Jews."[15] In d'Holbach's opinion, Christianity is a collection of "unconnected fables, senseless dogmas, puerile ceremonies, and notions borrowed from the Chaldeans, Egyptians, Phoenicians, Grecians, and Romans."[16]

Prosper Alfaric compares Jesus to Osiris, Attis, and Mithra.[17] Sylvain Maréchal compares him to Bacchus (also known as Dionysus), and Peter Jensen sees the Gospels as a remake of the epic of Gilgamesh.[18] Quite a mixed bag of comparisons! It is important to note that the allegedly copied texts are not the same from one critic to the next. We can also point out that no one who read the Gospels at the time they were written mistook them for mythological stories. And even the Jews who were in conflict with the first Christians never denied Jesus' existence.[19]

More fundamentally, the *methodology* behind these theses is completely defective. It has been called *parallelomania* because it tends to invent parallels where none exist historically. Consider these words from Prosper Alfaric:

He [the Christ] took the best from each one: sensational healings from Asclepius, specific details from the last supper of Mithra, as well as his birth date of December 25. He borrowed the betrayal of a loved one, and the pious attention of a weeping woman from Osiris.[20]

With this kind of methodology, and given the number of available sources, it wouldn't be hard to find similarities between anything and everything. I could use this type of parallelism to deny my own grandfather's existence, claiming that his whole life was a myth inspired by Disney movies!

He was born in France like Belle; his father died when he was young, similarly to Bambi's mom; he was raised by his widowed mother, just like Dumbo and the Aristocats. He is British on his grandmother's side, like Wendy and Peter Pan. He was raised in the Catholic faith, like the hunchback of Notre Dame, and had an amazing mind, like Aladdin's genie. His photographic memory was simply miraculous: As you can see, we are clearly dealing with a myth here.

Let's not forget that Dady went to the African desert during the war, which is a clear parallel with Simba in *The Lion King*. He was an amazing scientific inventor, like Merlin the wizard; and with his nuclear research, he made important contributions to his country's military defense, just like Mulan. He married a beautiful blonde, like Prince Charming did; and who can fail to see in him and his six sons a striking parallel with the seven dwarfs of *Snow White*, especially knowing he went on to become a "Doc" at the University of Poitiers?

This is all absurd, of course. But is my parallelomania any more ridiculous than that of the mythicists? When we carry this practice through to its logical conclusions, we can even deny the existence of the entire Jewish people, as Sylvain Maréchal does in *La Fable de Christ dévoilée* (The fable of Christ unveiled). He sees parallels between Moses and Bacchus, David and "Apollo of the Brahmins," and Solomon and "Libyan Jupiter."[21] His hypothesis is so bizarre that I have trouble even believing he's serious. At this point, we have entered the Twilight Zone.

The apostles' testimony

Finally, the mythicist thesis is particularly inadequate when it comes to explaining the testimonies given by the apostles and the Gospel writers. Were they trying to fool us? Were they themselves fooled? Michel Onfray sets forth some rather inconsistent theses concerning them:

> Were the authors of the New Testament conscious of this myth? I do not think so. It was neither conscious, nor deliberate, nor systematically thought out. Mark, Matthew, Luke, and John did not knowingly deceive. . . . *They were deceived,* for they said that what they believed was true and believed that what they said was true. None of them had encountered Jesus physically, but all credited this fiction with a real existence, in no way symbolic or metaphorical.[22]

The problem is that the authors all lay claim to eye-witness accounts in their writings, either their own or those of Jesus' disciples. John in particular refers to himself as "the disciple whom Jesus loved,"[23] and he along with Peter and James were especially close to Jesus.[24] Considering that the Gospel writers had nothing to gain and everything to lose by preaching Jesus' resurrection, Onfray knows he can't say they deliberately deceived us.

It also isn't reasonable to say they were honestly fooled about something as important as the very existence of their

Lord and Master. And if they were simply copying the pagan mythology of their times to create an epic hero, how could they remain honest in their assertions that these were true, historical accounts of the events depicted?

The mythicist thesis is also unreasonable given that the New Testament authors, first-century Jews who were faithful to the Torah, hated the pagan polytheism of the neighboring people in the region. It is quite improbable that they would have embraced idolatrous stories to concoct their own Christianized version "à la Jesus," all the while remaining faithful to the Old Testament Jewish faith.

Why, then, would they come up with such strange inventions? Prosper Alfaric simply says that the writers were "overtaken by fever,"[25] and they invented Jesus to complete the Old Testament.[26] But this doesn't answer the question of their sincerity or of why they would have lied if they were not sincere in their affirmation of Jesus' existence.

And what about the apostle Paul, who received a direct revelation from God that was later authenticated by Peter, James, and John in Jerusalem?[27] Charles Guignebert, who was radically skeptical of the Gospels' reliability and believed we know precious little about Jesus, at least concluded that Jesus' existence was *proven*—if by nothing else, by four of Paul's epistles: "Until we're convincingly shown otherwise, we will believe that, all questions of interpolation put aside, the four great Pauline epistles are authentic, and they suffice to prove the historical existence of Jesus."[28]

In conclusion, Jesus of Nazareth's existence is especially

well attested by historical sources, and it can only be rejected by means of a radical form of skepticism that obliterates our knowledge of antiquity. The quality of the sources doesn't justify such a radical view, which is based, instead, on a presupposition that the miracles recounted in the Gospels could not have occurred.

If, on the other hand, we're even a little bit open to the idea, the sources allow us to build an impressive case based on serious historical evidence. This case is not only favorable to Jesus' existence but also to his resurrection. Indeed, the historical data defending this event is remarkably positive.

The resurrection of Jesus of Nazareth

When evaluating historical sources concerning Jesus, from the standpoint of purely historical criticism, some facts are so well documented that they are affirmed by the vast majority of scholars, even atheists and critics of the Christian faith. Christians have no reason to limit themselves to facts that are unanimously believed, but it is remarkable that those are accepted even by critics. Here are some of the historical facts commonly accepted by even the most skeptical leading authorities on the question:

1. Jesus died by crucifixion under the watch of Roman soldiers.
2. Jesus was buried by Joseph of Arimathea in a nearby tomb.

3. On the Sunday after the crucifixion, the tomb was found empty by a group of women who were disciples of Jesus.
4. After Jesus' death, the disciples underwent a series of experiences where they at least believed they saw Jesus alive.
5. Jesus' disciples began to proclaim that Jesus was risen from the dead.[29]

No single fact, on its own, entails that Jesus rose from the dead. Atheists and skeptics accept them because they satisfy the criteria of historical authenticity. Most of these facts are supported by multiple independent sources, in texts that date back to a period close to the actual events, and some contain admissions that satisfy the criterion of embarrassment. For example, Joseph of Arimathea was a member of the Jewish Sanhedrin that condemned Jesus. Nonetheless, the New Testament tells us that he took care of Jesus' body and respectfully laid it in a tomb. We would expect Christians to be hostile toward the Sanhedrin, but the writers proclaim Joseph's noble gesture, probably because they were telling the truth.

In the same way, it would have been culturally embarrassing at the time that *women* discovered the empty tomb because a woman's testimony carried no weight. If the authors were making up the story, they probably would have attributed the discovery to a well-respected man, a close disciple like Peter, for example. Why would they admit that women were the ones who went to the tomb and found it empty?

Probably because that's what happened and they were simply telling the truth, whether it was convenient or not. (During my own study of Christianity, when I was still an atheist, I remember being struck by the fact that the sources I was evaluating were brutally honest in confessing the fallibility of the disciples—sometimes comically so.)

For these reasons and for others discussed in the academic literature, the vast majority of New Testament historians, whether Christian or not, attest to these historical facts.[30] So we are left asking the essential question: *What is the best explanation?*

Did Jesus only *appear* to be dead yet was still alive? Did the disciples go to the wrong tomb? Were they fooled by a villainous Jesus? Were his sightings merely hallucinations? Were the disciples coconspirators and liars? None of these explanations holds water; they have too many gaping holes.

It is difficult to challenge the historical truth of Jesus' death. The Romans were specialists in the art of execution, and Christ's death was verified by a Roman centurion. It was the centurion's job, and he would have been executed himself if he made a false declaration. Also, a half-dead Jesus couldn't have rolled away the stone to escape and then convinced the disciples that he was the risen Lord of glory, if he had been covered with bleeding wounds and at death's door.

The "wrong tomb" hypothesis does not align with Joseph of Arimathea's stature in the community. His tomb would have been well known and correctly marked. When the disciples started proclaiming Jesus' resurrection, their enemies could easily have gone to the correct tomb in order to disprove the disciples' claims. Moreover, even if the "wrong tomb" hypothesis might explain the finding of an empty tomb, it doesn't explain the multiple postmortem sightings and the disciples' belief in Christ's resurrection.

According to Baron d'Holbach, Jesus tricked the disciples. They were, "by their own concession, . . . ignorant and unlearned men, and, consequently, liable to be imposed upon by the artifices of a dexterous impostor."[31] This theory doesn't explain how, much less why, Jesus would have come up with such a hoax. D'Holbach also wrongly presupposes that the disciples were all naïve and stupid. This was certainly not the case with Matthew, a tax collector; James, leader of the church in Jerusalem; or Paul, a Pharisee educated by Gamaliel who makes such masterful use of logic in his letters.[32] In short, this hypothesis doesn't hold up.

Were the disciples hallucinating when they saw the living Jesus after his death? Ernest Renan tries to explain: "Such was the impression he had left in the hearts of his disciples and of a few devoted [women], that during some weeks more it was as if he were living and consoling them."[33]

Renan offers an accusation couched in a compliment concerning Mary Magdalene, whose "strong imagination . . . played in this circumstance an important part. Divine power of love! Sacred moments in which the passion of one possessed gave to the world a resuscitated God!"[34]

The hallucination theory suffers from other insurmountable problems as well. First, the *post-mortem* sightings were reported by different sorts of people, at different times, and in different contexts.[35] It is unlikely they all had the same hallucination. Then, a hallucination cannot explain the fact that the disciples believed in Christ's bodily *resurrection*. They may have thought God gave them a vision of Jesus, but to come to the conclusion that he was risen from the dead, they would have had to have had physical interactions with him, which is exactly what the Gospel sources affirm. On top of that, hallucinations don't explain the empty tomb.

So were the disciples a band of plotting charlatans? Baron d'Holbach seems to think so.

> Were those witnesses disinterested? No; it was, undoubtedly, their chief interest to support those miracles, upon which were suspended the divinity of their master, and the truth of the religion they were endeavoring to establish.[36]

These conspiracy theories are no more valid than the others we've examined. The disciples had nothing to gain and everything to lose by establishing Christianity. Several were persecuted, and some even executed, after preaching about the Resurrection. A sincere person who is mistaken might sacrifice his life for a false theory but not for something that he *knows* to be untrue. What's more, the disciples couldn't have stolen the body because it was guarded day and night by Roman soldiers.

And finally, the critics must choose: Either the disciples were fools and idiots, or they were liars and coconspirators. Once again, we find ourselves up against a wall.

None of these explanations holds water. The only probable explanation, and the only one that aligns with the historical data, is the one the disciples gave: God raised Jesus from the dead.

So what?

My conversations with Robert, my own thought processes, and my reading of the New Testament brought me to the conclusion that the Gospels were reliable. I decided it was intellectually reasonable to believe the authors' versions of the events surrounding the life, death, and resurrection of Jesus. So was that it? Was I a Christian now? Is the story of my conversion over and you can just close the book? Not at all. Why not? Because, in reality, the Christian faith is not simply intellectual belief in God's existence and Jesus' resurrection. Yes, these affirmations are necessary, but they are not *sufficient*. There was still an important element missing from my becoming a Christian, and it wouldn't be long before I found it.

During my personal research, I followed along in the little Bible reading booklet that Robert had written. I recorded my endless questions in the margins of the pages. Many of my questions were answered during my conversations with Robert, but one kept coming up, over and over again: *Why did Jesus have to die on the cross?*

I was ready intellectually to accept the fact that the events described in the Gospels really happened, but even if they had, what did it have to do with my life today? What was the connection between Jesus, who died on a cross two thousand years ago, and my present life?

The answer finally came, but not in the way I was hoping. Without telling me, Robert had started praying that something would happen in my life, something quite unpleasant for me but absolutely necessary.

At the same time, my unbelieving prayers began to change, and I began praying more like this: "God, I'm beginning to believe you exist; but if you do, you'll have to reveal yourself to me even more clearly. I don't want to commit to you lightly and end up looking like a fool. If you're there, show me your truth in a powerful way."

I don't know if I expected the skies to open, a light to fall on me, like in the movies, and a loving voice to say, "Welcome, my son," but that isn't what happened.

Instead, God did something much less theatrical but also much more brutal: He reactivated my conscience.

Where the Head Went,
the Heart Followed

• • •

In short, the ministers of religion furnish to the most
profligate men the means of diverting from their own
heads the thunderbolt that should strike their crimes,
with the promise of a never-fading happiness.

BARON D'HOLBACH

"GUILLAUME, LET'S TALK A LITTLE BIT about your religious background," Robert said. "Before you became an atheist, you
were a practicing Catholic, right? What do you remember
from that time?"

"Not much," I replied without enthusiasm. "I mostly recall
being bored and feeling like I was wasting my time at Mass or
in catechism class. As far as rituals go, I was baptized, did my
First Communion and my confirmation. I also recall having
to go before the priest once or twice during a retreat or some
other event while I was in middle school, where I was asked to
'confess' to the priest and receive what he called 'reconciliation.'
Apparently, we were supposed to tell the priest all the bad things
we'd done and then he forgave us. I really didn't see the point."

"So what sins did you confess?"

"Ha, good question! Each time I went to confession, I told the priest I wasn't sure I'd really done anything bad, but that some people told me I was *proud*. That seemed like a good answer to the priest's questions since pride wasn't really too serious an offense. He could do his little ritual, forgive me for my 'sin' (which I didn't really think I'd committed), and everything would be fine. I could leave knowing that I was a pretty good guy. Yeah, I'd say that 'a little bit of pride' was what I typically confessed."

I expected Robert to gloss over my answer and sweep my ridiculous "sin" under the rug. But instead, with his kind voice and American accent, he said, "I see. You know, there's hardly anything more offensive to the Lord than pride. It's a stench in the Lord's nostrils."

This exchange occurred during one of my very first conversations with Robert in his office—and I must say, it woke me up. I was unaccustomed to such honesty, but I found it refreshing. Clearly, he wasn't going to walk on eggshells just to make me happy. I soon discovered that the Bible doesn't mince words either when it comes to pride, calling it "an abomination to the LORD."[1]

All that aside, I wasn't entirely convinced I was a proud person, and I really didn't feel guilty about anything I had done. If I didn't feel bad about the awful way I had treated my girlfriends and some of my closest friends, a conversation with a pastor wasn't going to convince me of my abominable character. I saw myself as a nice young man, with a good sense of humor, intelligent, athletic, polite, passionate, a good musician, etc. I'm telling you: I was a good guy!

This lack of self-awareness explains the shock to my system when God reactivated my conscience.

I had been suppressing "one little detail" from my past by continually pushing it to the back of my mind until I thought it had disappeared. In truth, it was a disgusting moral violation that went far beyond anything else I had done. I had hidden it from everyone by lying profusely to my loved ones and to myself. But now it came roaring back with a vengeance and I could no longer push it aside.

At about the same time I was starting to look into Christianity, I had cheated on Vanessa several times with a French woman who was also in a committed relationship. There were additional, amplifying circumstances—I won't go into the sordid details—but I had been able to bury the memory under a mountain of lies and live as if it had never happened. That is, until God struck me down with the realization of my guilt.

When the memory of what I had done came back, it was so vivid it made me physically ill. With my conscience reawakened, I clearly saw the abominable nature of my sin, and I was crippled by guilt.

My epiphany

In our culture, we often think of guilt as something negative. We see it as an unhealthy feeling that we need to do away with in order to feel good about ourselves. I would agree that it's unhealthy for someone to feel a false sense of guilt (which may simply be a manifestation of *regret*, not culpability), but true guilt is intended to drive us toward repentance.

When these memories came back to haunt me, I *felt* guilty because I *was* guilty! And the pain was unbearable. It was well deserved but devastating. I was afflicted.

I can still see myself, alone in my apartment, lying on the floor and lamenting, *What have I done? Oh, what have I done? I can't take it back. I can't erase the past. I can't start over. I've ruined everything. I'm such a jerk. I wanted to have a good, healthy romantic relationship with a wonderful woman from America, but instead I had to dive back into my lies and my cheating. Why? Why? Why?*

In the middle of all that pain and regret, a shard of light broke through. I finally had the answer to my nagging question: "Why did Jesus have to die on the cross?"

He died for *me*.

The Bible says that Jesus "bore our sins in his body on the tree, that we might die to sin and live to righteousness. By his wounds you have been healed."[2] Now I understood the weight of all that. Now I understood the sacrifice.

That guilt I was feeling? The Bible affirmed it. I had even read about it in my own research: "No one is righteous—not even one. . . . No one does good, not a single one."[3]

In God's system of justice, anyone who has done evil, anyone who has sinned, anyone who is guilty, deserves condemnation and eternal separation from God's presence. But Jesus, who had no moral debt of his own, having lived a sinless life, came to pay *our* debt on the cross, so that we could be freely forgiven.

This is the incredible message of the Bible: Salvation and eternal life are free gifts, paid for entirely by Jesus himself, and simply given to those who will accept his sacrifice on their behalf and put their faith in him.

"This is how God loved the world: He gave his one and only Son, so that everyone who believes in him will not perish but have eternal life."[4]

When someone asks, "What must I do to go to heaven?" the most common response is along the lines of, "You must do good so that your good works will outweigh your evil deeds." Many people seem to assume that good works will tip the scales in their favor and bring a positive outcome on Judgment Day.

The problem, according to the Bible, is that *no one* can do enough good to outweigh the bad. Not you, not me, not anyone.

The prophet Isaiah confirms that even our best actions and self-generated righteousness, compared to God's perfect and holy standard, are "nothing but filthy rags."[5] Jesus says we "must be perfect, as your heavenly Father is perfect."[6] Good luck with that!

If moral perfection is a prerequisite for eternal life in heaven, the question the disciples asked Jesus makes perfect sense: "Then who can be saved?"[7] His answer confirms their suspicions: "With man it is impossible, but not with God. For all things are possible with God."[8]

Christian teaching is counterintuitive: No one can *earn* eternal life. There is nothing we can do to save ourselves; only God can do it. But this is the Good News of the Christian message: God accomplished it in the person of Jesus of Nazareth. He died for us and rose again, so that all who believe in him have their sins forgiven and receive eternal life.

Just like that.

Freely.

Salvation is by *faith* in the finished work of Jesus, not by our meager good works.

Jesus taught this quite clearly: "Whoever believes in him [God's Son] is not condemned, but whoever does not believe is condemned already, because he has not believed in the name of the only Son of God."[9]

Paul the apostle says it this way: "For the wages of sin is death, but the free gift of God is eternal life in Christ Jesus our Lord."[10]

This is the famous "Good News" that Christians call "the gospel."

"For by grace you have been saved through faith. And this is not your own doing; it is the gift of God, not a result of works, so that no one may boast."[11]

In my pain, the message of grace and forgiveness hit me like a ton of bricks. Here was the connection between the death of Jesus in the past and my present life. Jesus had been condemned to death so that I could be forgiven.

In a flash of sudden self-awareness, my life experience lined up with the intellectual understanding I had acquired through my research of the Bible. And I finally yielded. On the threshold of Christian faith, I prayed, "God, I give up. You've got me. For a while now, I haven't known what to think about you. But I'm ready to accept the fact of your existence and the free gift of forgiveness offered in Jesus. Forgive me, rebuild my life; do with me what you will."

I stepped across the threshold privately, timidly. But I knew I would have to walk the talk publicly. Now that I had confessed my sin to God, did I also have to confess it to Vanessa? If so, I would need to do it in person—across the Atlantic, about 3,600 miles outside my comfort zone. As it happened, I had already purchased an airline ticket to New York City. It was time to go see Vanessa for the first time in her home environment.

Taking the plunge

"Don't say anything, Guillaume. She doesn't need to know. Turn the page and forget the past. Don't ruin everything."

In a nutshell, that is the advice I got from everyone I asked as my December trip to New York approached. Everyone except Robert. He didn't get a chance to give me *any* advice because I didn't talk to him about anything before I left. Not about my guilt; not about my nascent Christian faith. I wasn't ready to admit everything to him, yet I felt the need to talk to *someone* about my actions. I mentioned the affair to some of my good friends. They all told me to keep it a secret and try to build a good relationship with Vanessa without the weight of the past, since it would almost certainly ruin our relationship.

However, my conscience kept bothering me, and it was increasingly difficult to keep things quiet. I didn't know what to do.

With my mind and heart full of conflicting emotions, I took off from Paris. I had eight hours alone on the airplane to think about what I would do and say once I arrived in New York City. But more than just the latest events were on my mind. Vanessa and I needed to talk about our future together. If things were going to work out between us, it would be up to me to move to New York. I already spoke English, whereas Vanessa didn't know a word of French. It would be easier for me to find a job in New York than for her to find one in Paris. So it was up to me to either take the plunge and move to New York, leaving behind everything I knew, or admit my repeated unfaithfulness and my lies, break her heart, and return to Paris alone. Sitting in the airplane, alone with my thoughts, one thing was certain: I was on the verge of doing something that would radically affect the rest of my life.

The feelings of inner conflict followed me off the plane. Vanessa had organized the perfect week for me to discover New York, the city of superlatives. It was totally different from anything I'd ever experienced—so much larger than life, with all the skyscrapers and the extravagant activity everywhere you go. But combining the euphoria of discovering this new place with my girlfriend, whom I'd missed for so many months, and my strong inner feelings of guilt had my stomach in a perpetual knot.

The extreme tension continued to grow throughout the week while I was discovering Times Square by night; the amazing Christmas decorations on Sixth Avenue; the giant Christmas tree in front of the famous ice-skating rink at Rockefeller Center; the sounds and sights of Christmas at Saks Fifth Avenue; the New York City Ballet's presentation of *The Nutcracker* at Lincoln Center; my first cheesecake in a restaurant in Little Italy; and even a helicopter flight over Manhattan!

I also met someone very important to Vanessa during my vacation, when I was finally introduced to her beloved pastor, Vincent Salonia. He and his wife, Grace, invited us over for dinner. I had heard so much about Pastor Vinny that I was eager to see what he looked like. That evening, I met a stocky, Italian-American man in his fifties with a big black mustache and a warm smile. He was also an amazing musician. In his younger days, he had played in a rock band, traveling across America on a tour bus and playing in a different town every night. During this time, he had become a Christian and was delivered from drugs. With a big smile, he told me that knowing Jesus was a much better high than drugs had ever been.

Vinny and Grace welcomed me with open arms, and we became fast friends. Vinny took an interest in me and began asking questions, eager to know where I stood in my reflections on God. I answered with a major understatement: "I'm somewhat interested."

Vinny had studied theology in depth during his years as a pastor, and he had the heart of a teacher. He was obviously thrilled to talk to me about God, Jesus, the Bible, and the gospel. His excitement was contagious, but I ended up falling asleep as a result of jet lag (not at all because I wasn't interested in what he was saying). We got together several times during my visit.

As the week went on, my conflicted feelings grew. The joy of discovering New York was steadily succumbing to the guilt that was eating me alive. God's existence and the pertinence of the gospel were also becoming more real to me. It was obvious that I was guilty before God; yet at the same time, I had accepted the fact that my salvation depended on faith in Jesus, not on my own actions. I was ready to put a seal on that reality by making a public confession of my faith.

"Vinny, now that I believe in Jesus, what are the next steps for a new Christian like me? What is the protocol? What should I do now?"

"Well, once you are saved, you should be baptized. The believer is lowered into the water and comes back up to proclaim his faith in Jesus and to identify with Christ's death and resurrection."

"Okay, so what do I have to do to make that happen? What are the conditions?"

"There are no conditions, other than repenting of your sins and believing in Jesus. It's very simple, really. We read about the first Christian baptisms in the Bible, in the book of the Acts of the Apostles. The message that was proclaimed after Jesus' death was pretty straightforward: 'Repent, believe, and be baptized.'"

"I see. So what's holding me back? Is there any reason that I shouldn't be baptized tomorrow or even today?"

I could see he was caught off guard by the directness of my question.

"Well, umm, I guess there's no reason not to do it. Absolutely! You want to do it? You want me to baptize you tomorrow?"

"Yes."

That same evening, we invited some people from Vinny's church who were available to come the next day.

The following afternoon, Vinny arrived at Vanessa's apartment with his guitar. We sang two or three songs and then he baptized me in the bathtub. With my long legs, I hardly fit, but it was the perfect metaphor for a coffin and a rebirth. My former life was buried and my new life in Christ began. I now identified with the death and resurrection of Jesus.

As I came up out of the water, I was filled with peace. Just like Jesus promised, all my sins were forgiven through faith in him. I was calm. My guilt was gone, and I was at peace with God. Once again, the words of the Bible penetrated my heart: "Therefore, since we have been justified by faith, we have peace with God through our Lord Jesus Christ."[12]

Too easy?

It's not hard to imagine the objections that will surely arise from some who read my story.

"Guillaume, isn't it all too easy? By your own admission, you did some really awful things. And now, just by 'accepting Jesus,' you wiped your conscience clean? You had nothing left to be ashamed of? All was well?"

I not only understand this objection, but I would be thrilled to hear it. If the message of the gospel seems shocking to you, it's because it *is* shocking. And there's nothing I can say to change it or make it more palatable. May this objection come up every time I talk to a skeptic! It would prove that I've gotten my message across and that my story conveys the same message taught by Jesus and his disciples. It's not surprising that in proclaiming this Good News of salvation through Christ, his disciples came up against the same objection. Paul anticipated it in his letter to the Romans: "What shall we say then? Are we to continue in sin that grace may abound? By no means!"[13]

There's no way to avoid pushback when we announce something of this magnitude. There's nothing you can do to remove your own sin. Jesus already accomplished it on your behalf. That's why Christians call it the Good News.

Christians who are truly repentant won't *want* to sin anymore because their hearts have been changed. They will live for God and naturally desire to fight against sin. They know their good works won't *save* them, but good works will be the natural *result* of the incredible gift they have freely received.

The epistle of James teaches the same thing: If we *say* we have faith but have no good works as a result, then our faith isn't real; it's *dead*.[14] True repentance and true faith in Christ will radically change our lives. Good works will be the natural product of this faith. Free forgiveness entails a radical change in the lives of those who receive it.

Victor Hugo illustrates this brilliantly in *Les Misérables* with the beautiful contrast between Jean Valjean's repentance and Javert's suicide. One happens at the beginning of the book and the other at the end, but both men freely receive forgiveness.

Valjean, who stole silverware from the church, is forgiven by the priest who could have sent him to die in prison. Instead, the priest offers Valjean freedom—and two more silver candlesticks! This softens Valjean's heart and dramatically propels him into an honest life, restored and filled with a generosity motivated by thankfulness.

Javert, on the other hand, is sentenced to death by insurgents in a reversal of circumstances at the end of the book. Javert is spared by Valjean and allowed to escape. But this unconditional forgiveness upsets his rigid idea of justice such that he cannot accept it. He throws himself off a bridge into the Seine River.

Here are two amazing illustrations of the power of freely offered forgiveness. The one who humbly accepts it goes on to live a beautiful life, while the one who cannot accept it is lost forever. A changed life does not *merit* forgiveness, but free forgiveness is so powerful that it will assuredly change the life of the person who accepts it.

So is salvation by faith *too easy?* Yes and no. Yes because it's a free gift. It doesn't depend on our good works: It's the *Good News.* On the other hand, no, because accepting it requires us to admit our need for it. And even this much isn't easy for some. Ernest Renan explains, in all sincerity, why he never felt the need:

> I, as a man of culture, do not find any evil in myself, and I am impelled spontaneously towards what seems to me the most noble. If all others had as much culture as myself, they would all, like myself, be incapable of doing an evil act.[15]

Oh, if only everyone were as noble and good as I am!

I probably wouldn't have put it that way, but Renan's statement isn't far from my prideful lack of self-awareness at the time I met Robert. I can still hear his uncompromising words: "There's hardly anything more *offensive*. . . . It's a *stench* in the Lord's nostrils . . ."

Jesus himself told a story using similar words:

> Two men went up into the temple to pray, one a Pharisee and the other a tax collector. The Pharisee, standing by himself, prayed thus: "God, I thank you that I am not like other men, extortioners, unjust, adulterers, or even like this tax collector. I fast twice a week; I give tithes of all that I get." But the tax collector, standing far off, would not even lift up his eyes to heaven, but beat his breast, saying, "God, be merciful to me, a sinner!" I tell you, this man went down to his house justified, rather than the other.

For everyone who exalts himself will be humbled,
but the one who humbles himself will be exalted.[16]

The proud religious man who thought of himself as good
is condemned. The repentant sinner is forgiven. He admits his
sin, throws himself on God's mercy, and receives free salvation.
His heart is filled with gratitude. That is what salvation by faith
looks like.

Saved by . . . blind faith?

Understanding the gospel message of salvation by faith, by trust-
ing in Jesus alone, allows us to rectify another common misunderstanding found in the writings of many skeptical thinkers.
A good number of them criticize the call to *faith*, describing it
as a kind of blind belief at cross-purposes with knowledge; as
unreasonable or even irrational. Let's look at some statements that
reveal an utter—and sometimes comical—misunderstanding of
what Christians mean when they speak of faith.

Faith, which is a blind belief that serves as a
foundation for all religions, is only a principle of
errors, illusions, and deceptions.[17]

JEAN MESLIER

Faith consists in believing not what seems true, but
what seems false to our understanding.[18]

VOLTAIRE

[Faith] consists in an impossible conviction of the revealed doctrines and absurd fables which the Christian religion commands its disciples to believe. Hence it appears that this virtue exacts a total renunciation of reason, and impracticable assent to improbable facts, and a blind submission to the authority of priests, who are the only guarantees of the truth of the doctrines and miracles that every Christian must believe under penalty of damnation.[19]

BARON D'HOLBACH

Faith will always be in inverse ratio to vigour of mind and intellectual culture.[20]

ERNEST RENAN

The refrain repeats itself: Christians have faith because they don't know any better and because they don't think for themselves. This, of course, is worlds apart from what Christians mean by "faith."

Robert explained this to me during our conversations. He used a simple but effective illustration: Visualize a small child standing on a table and throwing himself into his father's arms before the father even stretches out his arms to catch him. The child has no absolute certainty or scientific proof that he will be safe. But he *trusts* his father. He is not irrational; he *knows* that his father is trustworthy, and he has faith in him. Similarly, Christian faith is not contrary to reason. It is not ignorance or a blind leap of faith in the dark. It is a settled *trust* in God, rooted in his character and faithfulness, and justified by reason and experience.

Ultimately, that was how I experienced my conversion and my acceptance of salvation through faith in Jesus. My mind accepted Christianity's rationality and the trustworthiness of the Gospels. My heart knew its need of salvation. And I received forgiveness by faith in Jesus.

But let's get back to New York. The final evening of my vacation was coming up soon, and I still needed to decide what to do about Vanessa. That afternoon, I asked to see Vinny. I really needed some advice, and he agreed to meet with me.

Confession

I didn't start by telling Vinny I had a dark secret to confess to Vanessa. Before I got around to that, I wanted to talk to him about something else that was bothering me. I had already noticed it from a distance, but now, having spent a solid week with Vanessa on her home turf, I believed she was emotionally fragile, overly sensitive, and prone to jealousy. It was understandable, given her difficult past, but I was troubled about the prospect of leaving everything I knew in France to try to build a life with her under those circumstances.

When I shared my concerns with Vinny, he didn't try to contradict me on these points. He told me he loved Vanessa unconditionally, with all of his heart—that she was like a daughter to him; but he also agreed that she struggled with things that could deeply affect our relationship. He explained that what a healthy marriage needs is unity, harmony, mutual forgiveness, and peace. As we talked, it became apparent to me that Vanessa and I weren't meant to be together.

Inwardly, I was relieved to think that, if we broke up, I wouldn't have to admit my unfaithfulness to her. If we weren't going to make a go of it anyway, why should I tell her the sordid details of my life? I thanked Vinny for his time and his advice, and I decided I would break up with Vanessa that evening.

When I dropped the news on her, she broke down in tears. I was heartbroken to see her in such pain. In the midst of her tears, she couldn't understand what was happening, and kept asking me, "Why? Why now? Did something else happen? What are you hiding?"

She became increasingly emotional, and I was at a breaking point myself. Seeing her pain, I realized that I really didn't want to break up with her. But in order to stay together, I would have to break her heart again by confessing my secret.

I just couldn't do it. We were both crying, and she kept repeating, "What is it that you can't tell me? What are you hiding?"

It was just too much pressure. I was exhausted by my lies; the truth had to come out. Finally, at my wits' end, I gave up. I did it. I told her everything—with all the sordid details. I left nothing out. I got everything off my chest. Whatever happened next, I at least knew that I would be living in the light of the truth.

At this point in the story, maybe you're expecting a happy ending—one that would depict God's grace as revealed in the gospel. As Paul said, "Be kind to one another, tenderhearted, forgiving one another, as God in Christ forgave you."[21]

In this imaginary scenario, after I admitted my sins, Vanessa—full of supernatural grace—would forgive me freely and I would enjoy the divine experience of forgiveness that I had already received from God. And Vanessa and I would live happily ever after.

Let's just say that the scene played out differently in real life. Vanessa took my confession very badly and went into an uncontrollable rage. She tried to hit me; she screamed at me, and she insulted me. Obviously, I deserved it, but it went on for hours until we both finally collapsed from exhaustion. We fell asleep in the early morning, just a few hours before I had to leave for the airport. It was clearly over between us, and it was not at all a good way for things to end.

As the sun began to rise, I put my suitcases in the car and glanced up at the house where so much had happened in such a short amount of time. We took off for the airport, saying almost nothing on the way. Vanessa had calmed down, but our polite, clipped conversation resembled that of two strangers who will never see each other again, sharing an elevator.

When we arrived at the terminal, I got out of the car and said goodbye. I was emotional, but I kept my composure. After the usual ordeal of getting through security, I boarded the plane that would take me back to my life in France. There

I was, absorbed in my own thoughts, trying to make sense of what was going on in my head and in my heart.

What a week! So many emotions! I needed to calm down and think about my future. In the midst of the pain surrounding the breakup, I found I also had to fight the temptation to let go of my faith. I knew that the success or failure of my relationship with Vanessa had nothing to do with the *truth* of Christianity. I was now convinced of that. The fact that Vanessa refused to forgive me wouldn't change my view of God's forgiveness. I was determined not to back away. My new life would not be in America, but I would be a Christian. Now I just needed to figure out what that would look like. I needed to get back to work and back to my music and volleyball. But I would do it as a believer in Jesus and as a single young adult living in Paris.

At least, that was the plan. But as I exited the airport in Paris, I noticed the little envelope on my telephone screen.

I had a new voicemail message.

10

Moves and Debates

● ● ●

He but ill deserves the title of philosopher, who has
not the courage to hear his opinions contradicted.

BARON D'HOLBACH

VANESSA HAD APPARENTLY RECOVERED from the night before.
She sounded tired, but the message she left was calm and well
thought out. She told me she was suffering, and it was really
hard for her, but she wanted to forgive me.

"I don't know what to think about *us*, and I don't know
if we can rebuild anything together, but I'm not angry anymore. I have to forgive you. I want to forgive you."

Her words comforted me somewhat on my way to work.
Yes, that's right, I flew all night and went straight from the
airport to the office. After a sleepless night and a seven-hour
flight, the return to reality was brutal. I felt like a zombie all
day, and it took me the rest of the week to get over my jet lag.

The next Sunday morning, I went back to Le Bon Berger for church and to see Robert. I had to tell him all that happened. He could tell I was at the end of my rope.

"Oh, Guillaume, you don't look so good. Are you all right?"

"No, I'm not. Robert. We have to talk. A lot of things have happened. I didn't tell you everything. I'm such a jerk."

"All right, let's talk right after the service. But you know what? I've been praying for this to happen."

What? What exactly has he been praying? That everything would go wrong?

No, not exactly. Once I related everything that had happened in New York, Robert explained to me with great compassion what he meant: He had prayed that I would confront my immorality. He'd prayed that God would shatter my pride and that I would discover the depth of my guilt and accept the forgiveness available to me through the work of Jesus Christ. Indeed, if I wanted to have eternal life in God's presence, as Christianity said I could, I had to admit I was a sinner. Robert knew that the only way I would do that was if I was in pain. He didn't want the pain for me, per se, but as a good pastor, he wanted me to be saved, and he was praying in that direction. That's tough love.

Vanessa and I spent a lot of time on the phone together over the next few days. We still had strong feelings for each other. She forgave me and said she wanted to try to work on our relationship—which she saw as evidence of God's redemptive work. She said we should start over from scratch, but this time on the right foot. We were so happy thinking about making up, and we really needed to see each other soon. She bought a ticket to come to France in February.

In my imagination, her arrival would be magical. I daydreamed about us running toward each other in slow motion, like in the movies. She would jump into my arms and we would spend a wonderful week rebuilding our relationship.

But when the day arrived, I got to the airport late. I didn't leave my apartment on time, and then I got stuck in traffic. While I was still on my way, Vanessa called me from a phone booth at Charles de Gaulle Airport. She was furious. When I finally got there, she glared at me and said I had ruined everything.

"You should have been here *early* with a bouquet of flowers. It's almost Valentine's Day!"

She pouted the whole way home. I was discouraged and felt she was really overreacting. But her behavior lined up with the explosive personality I had discovered in New York. She was happy as a clam when everything was going well, but her emotional swings were devastating when something went wrong.

The ups and downs continued over the next several days; but when I decided to focus on her good side, the rest of the week went much more smoothly. She went back to New York, and we found ourselves at a turning point. Another visit here or there wouldn't give me any more information about her. Her emotional fragility and her temper still concerned me, but I told myself that if we loved each other, we would be able to get over those hurdles and make it work. After all, she had forgiven me for doing something indescribably terrible. Couldn't I love her despite the intensity of her emotional torments? We certainly weren't guaranteed that our relationship would work, and I knew it wouldn't be easy, but I decided to persevere. I knew I was ready to make an extraordinary and romantic decision.

Let's go

"Vanessa? It's Guillaume. I can't stay on the phone too long because I'm driving, but I wanted to tell you something important: I'm on my way home from work, and I quit!"

"You what?"

"Yeah, I quit my job. I gave two months' notice, so I have exactly two months to find a job in New York, leave everything behind here in France, and start a new life with you."

She was thrilled. I had weighed the risk of not finding a job in New York and ending up still in France and unemployed. But because I worked in computer science in the finance industry, and New York is a major financial center, I figured it was the perfect place for me to find a job. Wall Street, here I come!

I quickly lined up an interview with a French bank headquartered near La Défense, just outside of Paris, for a position in software development in their commodities trading room in New York. A few days later, I got my answer: I got the job.

Victory! But now I had to draw the curtain on all my activities in France.

I said goodbye to my volleyball team and the band. Those were emotional days, given the years I had invested in both endeavors. It felt like I was losing an important part of myself—and probably forever. I would no longer be a musician in a band or part of a national championship level volleyball team.

But as I was sacrificing these two major segments of my life, I was looking forward to great new adventures in the US. My American girlfriend was a beautiful model, and I had a job on Wall Street. I was excited! I began imagining my triumphal entry in New York, but there was one slight hitch: I still needed to obtain an American visa, and that didn't go as planned.

The visa that my future employer was trying to get for me is called an E2 employee visa. The only way the American government will issue one of these visas is if the French company is considered a foreign investor on American soil and the employee is either an executive/manager/supervisor or has specialized knowledge and is considered an essential employee. In addition, there were several complicated financial hoops for the company to jump through to qualify as a "foreign investor."

Unfortunately, just when I handed in my application for the visa, the US Citizenship and Immigration Services decided to look into my future employer, to make sure they fit the criteria. Until the investigation was completed, all E2 applications were put on hold. I couldn't get any news, even from the American embassy in France.

"They will let us know when they know something" was all that the immigration lawyers could tell me. This situation lasted for months.

On top of that, having just bought my apartment, I couldn't resell it right away. So I put it up for rent and moved back home to live with my parents. When my two-month notice at work ended, I still didn't have any news about the visa. I started working for my new employer, in Paris, which entailed spending three hours a day on public transportation—between the bus, the train, and the subway.

Making matters even worse, Vanessa had rented an apartment for me in Manhattan, so I had an exorbitant lease payment on a New York apartment while still earning a French salary. This stressful situation went on for several months, and I felt completely helpless.

I spoke regularly with Robert and Vinny, and they were amazing sources of encouragement for me. From their respective sides of the Atlantic, they continued to answer my questions about Christianity and prayed that my visa would go through. I also spent a lot of time praying, and I began to wonder whether all these roadblocks were maybe a message from heaven. Was I supposed to give up on this crazy notion of moving to New York? It seemed too late for that! I had already burned all my bridges in France.

What was God doing in the midst of these challenges? What did he want me to do? I had become a Christian. I had confessed my sin to Vanessa, and she had forgiven me. I had been baptized. What more was there to do?

One day it occurred to me that there was one thing I hadn't yet done: I hadn't said anything to my parents about my conversion. I was bothered by this, and after a few days of reflection, I gathered up my courage and invited Maman to go out for pizza, just the two of us. At the restaurant, I told her about my conversion, my baptism, and my newfound Christian faith. She was very open to my news and even seemed happy about it. I felt lighthearted as we headed home.

Now that Maman was aware of the changes in my life, Papa would be too—after she told him later that evening. I was thrilled to share these important events with them, knowing that I could now live out my faith publicly.

The very next afternoon, I got a message from the embassy telling me that my visa had been accepted and I should come in and pick it up. *Incredible!*

The message said nothing about the visa holdup and offered no explanation of what had happened during those long weeks of waiting. Nothing. Just instructions for coming to the embassy to pick up my passport with the precious visa.

My employer's lawyers asked me if I had any further details, because there were about ten other people in the company who were also waiting for their E2 visas, who hadn't heard from the embassy. I was the only one who had been contacted. I went to the embassy on the designated day, they stamped my passport, and that was it.

Three days later, I was on a plane to JFK.

The American "dream"

I arrived in New York in June 2006. My new job was in midtown Manhattan, and I loved it. It was interesting and motivating, and I had great coworkers. They put me in charge of developing a new application for the trading floor, and when my superiors saw what I could do, they made me a supervisor, with one other developer reporting to me.

Not long after I arrived in New York, I received an email from a coworker back home who was still waiting for her E2 visa. She said, "Guillaume, I don't get it. We were both in the same situation, waiting for the same visa, and you're the only one who got it. What did you do to make it happen?"

With a smile on my face, I replied with a short email: "This might sound weird to you, but . . . I prayed." She never replied. Several weeks later, her visa finally came through and she joined us in New York. But she never mentioned it again.

Outside of work, things weren't going very well. Predictably, my relationship with Vanessa was very complicated. I expended enormous amounts of energy trying to make her happy, but to no avail. Her extreme emotions were the cause of many absurd arguments about anything and everything.

Despite all that, we got engaged, and I gave up my Manhattan apartment to save rent money. All my stuff was at Vanessa's, but because we weren't yet married, I slept on the sofa at Vinny and Grace's. I left their home early every morning and came back late at night. That alone was exhausting.

But the constant tension between Vanessa and me was the straw that broke the camel's back.

I hung in there as long as I could, but I was miserable. This unbearable situation went on for several months, but it seemed like an eternity to me. If I had been a bit more mature, I would have put a stop to it long before that. It should have been obvious that we couldn't get married under those conditions. But I had given up so much in France to pursue Vanessa that it was hard for me to admit that our relationship was a total failure. It was during one of our daily arguments that the question finally came up.

"This is ridiculous," I said. "Nothing is working. We can't live like this. What should we do? Should we break up?"

"Yes," Vanessa replied.

I didn't waste another minute. I gathered my things together and left.

This time it was for good. Our relationship was over.

Frequently asked questions and "the Jesus newsletters"

The breakup was difficult. Not because Vanessa had made me happy, far from it; but because I felt as if I had given up everything for her. I was across the ocean from my country, away from my French friends, and no longer with my band or my volleyball team. I had no social life, just work. What was I going to do with my life?

I had thought I was following God's call on my life when

I moved and left everything behind. All that for this? What was God trying to teach me by isolating me this way? I didn't have any answers to my questions.

That was when other questions started popping up—from my atheist friends in France. I had been exchanging emails with my brother and some of our mutual friends. I'm not sure how the conversation started, but somehow, we got onto the subject of religion. I took advantage of the opportunity to describe my newfound faith in God, and I explained the message of salvation by faith in the resurrected Jesus.

Of course, my friends and family answered with their own critiques, and I rapidly found myself in the middle of a series of written debates, me against everyone else. My friends in France brought up all kinds of objections, dealing mostly with salvation by faith and the question of creation versus evolution. I had to think about what they were saying and answer them, one by one.

A bit tongue in cheek, my friends started calling my emails "the Jesus newsletters." The title didn't bother me, so I decided to go with it. I wrote about a dozen such emails, which were my first attempts at formulating answers and arguments in favor of Christianity. Some of my answers hit the nail on the head, and others fell flat. When I read them now, fifteen years later, I'm embarrassed by the naiveté of some of my arguments. I was taking my first steps in the field of apologetics, and though I didn't know it at the time, it would become an important part of my life. But for the time being, I really enjoyed trying to give rational answers to their ideas while defending my own.

Let's look at some of the objections I heard, beginning with those tendered against the Christian message of salvation by faith in Jesus.

Too good to be condemned or too bad to be forgiven?

Of course, the first objection I received was the common question anticipated by the apostle Paul in Romans 6: "If we are saved by faith, why not continue to sin?" Typically, the questions were formulated like this: "Guillaume, it's not fair to say that someone can be saved and then go and sin every day without any regrets, just as long as he says a prayer at night." The answer I gave my friends was very similar to the one I detailed in the previous chapter. Good works don't save us, but true faith necessarily entails a changed heart, which leads to good works. If a purported believer does not repent, it's simply an indication that his or her faith is dead.

According to Jean Meslier, a perfect being *cannot* forgive sinners. "It would only be fair that an all-powerful and infinitely perfect being would punish all guilty and evil people and prevent them from carrying out their evil plans."[1] Therefore, if everyone is guilty of sin, we should all be condemned.

In absolute terms, this is true. Crime deserves its punishment. But for Christians, the price for sin *has already been paid* by Jesus on the cross. An exchange has taken place—a *substitution* between Jesus' fate and that of the sinners who believe in him.

Meslier doesn't offer an intelligent argument against this position; he merely insults it: "What madness, I say, to even have such a thought! I am at a loss for words to express the extent of such madness."[2] Alas, because words are needed to argue a point, a lack of words equals a lack of argument.

In the same vein, the complaint of some critics of Christianity is not that evil men are forgiven but that *not everyone* is forgiven. Some find it offensive that God would condemn or give a negative judgment on anyone. According to Baron d'Holbach, "The Christian represents his God as pouring out unbounded vengeance to all eternity."[3] That's not exactly a flattering description of God.

This is one of the more difficult hurdles to overcome when we talk about hell. The notion has been so caricatured that we imagine a sort of torture chamber filled with horned red demons with pointy tails carrying tridents. It is truly difficult to return to the biblical description.

It's true that the Bible speaks several times of a "lake of fire" to describe the final judgment.[4] But that is just one metaphor among others. The Bible also describes it as "the outer darkness," where there will be "weeping and gnashing of teeth"; as a casting out from the kingdom of God; and as "the second death."[5] Without any other details, it's hard to describe more precisely the biblical idea of hell. But whether or not these are metaphors, one thing seems clear about hell:

It's a horrible outcome for anyone who is condemned. This is why salvation in Christ is such good news.

On the other hand, this potential condemnation is sometimes the object of a moral counterargument. Bertrand Russell takes it upon himself to criticize Jesus on this subject: "There is one very serious defect to my mind in Christ's moral character, and that is that He believed in hell. I do not myself feel that any person who is really profoundly humane can believe in everlasting punishment."[6]

Interestingly, Jean Meslier gives the appropriate answer to Russell's statement: "An all-powerful and infinitely perfect being would punish all guilty and evil people."[7] Simply stated, those who would be subject to everlasting punishment are not innocent! Thus, if justice demands a punishment, it is not unjust to condemn the guilty person.

"But the punishment is too severe," Russell might say. In other words, does a finite sin deserve an infinite punishment? Voltaire also mentions this objection in his discussion of hell in his *Philosophical Dictionary*.[8]

Faced with this argument, Christians who understand hell as eternal have a choice between two possible answers:

1. We can emphasize that God is an infinite being, in order to defend the idea that rejecting an infinite God is in fact an infinite transgression. Even if the atheist doesn't agree, I don't see what argument he could offer to establish the incoherence of this position.

2. We can assert that there is no reason to believe that a sinner will cease sinning once he or she is dead. Once the sinner's heart is hardened and condemned, it keeps on rejecting God. Thus, the transgression has no end, and the punishment is not disproportionate. I find this answer to be the more powerful one.

These two answers are compatible with each other and can be given together. In conclusion, eternal judgment is entirely compatible with a perfectly just God.

Everyone?

We've answered the skeptics who complain that just anyone can be forgiven and also those who complain that not everyone is forgiven. Now let's answer the complaint that anyone *needs* to be forgiven in the first place.

According to the Bible, all people are born wicked and guilty in God's eyes. Hence the universal need for forgiveness through repentance and faith in Jesus. Voltaire did not agree, and he found this notion insulting: "It would be much more reasonable, much more noble, to say to men: 'You are all born good; see how dreadful it is to corrupt the purity of your being.'"[9]

There's just one problem: It would only be more reasonable and more noble if it were *true*. The idea that all men are sinners is not only biblical; it's also eminently plausible. It is one of the rare doctrines of Christian theology that can be observed empirically. All you have to do is look around you. Or better yet, take a look in the mirror. Even Bertrand Russell observes that "in the ordinary man and woman there is a certain amount of active malevolence, both special ill-will directed to particular enemies and general impersonal pleasure in the misfortunes of others."[10]

If this is true, Voltaire objected, then the problem also affects Christians:

> We are told that human nature is essentially perverse;
> that man is born a child of the devil, and wicked.
> Nothing can be more injudicious; for thou, my friend,
> who preachest to me that all the world is born perverse,
> warnest me that thou art born such also, and that I
> must mistrust thee as I would a fox or a crocodile.[11]

Exactly! As Christians, we admit that we are not excluded from the ranks of sinners. We don't claim to have access to heaven because we are *good* but because we are *forgiven*. The debate is null and void: Christians are sinners, and Voltaire isn't telling us anything new when he says, "Thou art born such also."

Voltaire also criticizes the idea that we are all sinners from birth, even those who seem to be the most wicked among us: "Man is not born wicked; he becomes so, as he becomes sick."[12] He goes on to explain his point of view, using an experiment. I don't believe he was trying to be funny, but if you are a parent, as I am, you'll probably read this with a smirk on your face:

Assemble all the children of the universe; you will
see in them only innocence, mildness, and fear; if
they were born wicked, mischievous, and cruel, they
would show some signs of it, as little serpents try to
bite, and little tigers to tear. But nature not having
given to men more offensive arms than to pigeons
and rabbits, she cannot have given them an instinct
leading them to destroy.[13]

I've never read a biography of Voltaire, but I think I'm safe
in assuming that he never had children. I have five young children of my own, *whom I love with all my heart*. But I can assure
you, dear Voltaire, that I've seen the *signs* you mentioned.

We've seen that the Christian message of salvation stands
up against the philosophers' criticism. Now let's take a look
at another major objection that was forcefully brought up by
the readers of the Jesus newsletters. They pressed the scientific question concerning creation and evolution.

The challenge of evolution

As one of my friends put it: "Religion asks us to question the
theory of evolution, which I believe to be proven. According
to modern biology, life appeared through a long evolutionary
process and not by the work of some biblical God who created
the world." In other words, if you believe in God, you must
reject the scientific view of the origin of life. So what should we
believe? Is evolution an insurmountable problem for Christians?

In order to evaluate this question, we must understand where the alleged problem lies. In order to refute theism on the basis of biology, the atheist must affirm two things:

1. The theory of evolution is incompatible with the thesis of creation, and
2. The theory of evolution is true.

If these two premises are true, then the creation thesis is indeed false. In response, Christians have a choice: They can reject the first premise, or the second, or both. Let's see what that entails in each case.

The first option is to reconcile evolution and creation. In order to do this, we can simply point out that the theory of evolution, in and of itself, does not necessitate atheism. It's perfectly possible to envision a creator God deciding to use the process of evolution, providentially directing its path to produce all the living beings he wants to create. In this scenario, God remains the primary cause of all life and retains his position as Creator, while allowing the theory of evolution to be true.

This might seem like a coherent answer, but it's not that simple. Christians do not seek to merely defend "the idea of creation." We affirm creation *as taught in the Bible*. Consequently, we must admit that, at least on the surface, the first few chapters of the book of Genesis *seem* incompatible with the standard theory of evolution. So where do we go from here?

Reconciliation . . . and rebuttal

Christians who want to affirm the theory of evolution might reason this way: The creation account in Genesis 1 and 2, when taken *literally*, seems incompatible with the standard theory of evolution. But it's not meant to be taken literally. Each text must be interpreted in the proper manner, and perhaps the first two chapters of Genesis should be understood to contain a more *poetic, illustrative*, and *metaphorical* teaching than a biology textbook does. The underlying message of these chapters is that God created all things and made man and woman "in his own image."[14] However, it wasn't his intent to give us a specific and scientific rendering of how creation came about. Now, we must tread lightly here. We're not talking about using modern science to twist our biblical interpretation, and we must insist that all Bible interpretations are not equal. We must study the text and interpret it *properly*. But the Genesis account contains several elements that are undoubtedly poetic, and therefore, it would be justifiable, and certainly not irrational, to interpret it as imagery.

That being said, let's take a look at the second premise and ask the fundamental question: Is the standard theory of evolution true? Given the scientific evidence, are Christians forced to agree that life on Earth developed according to the theory of evolution? Not at all. Today, many people assume that evolution is an absolutely unshakable fact that is only rejected by brainless religious fanatics, especially in America.

Given this context, I am very aware that I am exposing myself to ridicule as I voice a bit of skepticism. But ridicule never killed anyone, and mocking is not a rebuttal. Ernest Renan notes that "the jester has the immense advantage of being dispensed from furnishing proofs."[15] No one should be satisfied by such an exemption, so let's look at the question to see whether people who reject evolution truly deserve to be mocked. Renan adds that "the first step in the philosophical career is to become proof against ridicule."[16] Allow me, therefore, to become this proof and to insist that the standard theory of evolution is far from incontestable. It should be on the defensive.

First of all, we must observe that life on earth *appears* to be the fruit of intelligent design. This starting point is agreed upon by everyone, including atheist evolutionists like Richard Dawkins, who says that biology is "the study of complicated things that *give the appearance of* having been designed for a purpose."[17] Francis Crick asserts that "biologists must *constantly* keep in mind that what they see was not designed, but rather evolved."[18] This constant intellectual effort is definitely necessary when we listen to Jacques Monod speak of the translation process of DNA in each of our cells:

> The highly mechanical and even "technological"
> aspect of the translation process merits attention. The
> successive interactions of the various components
> intervening at each stage, leading to the assembly,
> residue by residue, of a polypeptide upon the surface
> of the ribosome, like a milling machine which

notch by notch moves a piece of work through to completion—all this inevitably recalls an assembly line in a machine factory.[19]

It's easy to see why Christians claim that these systems *seem* to be the result of intelligent design because they *are* the result of intelligent design.

The theory of evolution came on the scene to offer an *alternative* explanation for the obvious appearance of design. But what exactly does Charles Darwin's theory of evolution proclaim? First, it suggests that all living species come from a single, original, common ancestor. According to Darwin, they evolved over time, from generation to generation, taking different directions, changing gradually, and finally separating into the different species that we see today. All these elements are included in the theory of evolution.

But that's not all. Darwin additionally suggests a *mechanism* that directs the entire process. To what end? To explain how all the extremely complex living species we see today could have obtained this highly functional complexity without an intelligent creator behind the scenes. This mechanism is known as "natural selection" coupled with "random mutations."

When cells reproduce, they sometimes mutate (by a process we now know to be a copy error at the genetic level). Through a series of random genetic mutations, one individual member of a species may accidentally develop an original biological trait. If this mutation is useless or harmful to the individual, it will probably be lost naturally at the organism's death or at the death of its descendants. But if it provides an advantage that allows the individual to survive more successfully than others in its given environment, the organism will be more likely to live a longer life and reproduce, thereby passing these new mutated genes on to its offspring.

These descendants, possessing the same genetic advantage, will be more likely to survive and reproduce, while other members of the species will slowly die off and be eliminated by natural selection. Voilà! Given enough time for the process to repeat itself, the theory goes, it would explain the presence of today's varied and complex species, which have successfully adapted to their environments. All this without the work of an intelligent creator.

This ingenious mechanism is possible in theory. But the real question is not "Is it *possible?*" but, rather, "Is it *true?*" Is that really how all the different species came to be? Or were they designed specifically by an intelligent creator? Atheist supporters of the theory of evolution are often happy to defend the *possibility* of the evolution of organisms, and they act as if that's enough to establish its truth. If evolution is possible, we don't need God in order to explain living species. But this line of reasoning is invalid. By presupposing naturalism in this case, the atheists exclude *a priori* the hypothesis of divine creation. Jacques Monod affirms this quite openly:

> The cornerstone of the scientific method is the postulate that nature is objective. In other words, the *systematic* denial that "true" knowledge can be got at by interpreting phenomena in terms of final causes—that is to say, of "purpose."[20]

Obviously, with that kind of presupposition, the practitioners of Monod's "scientific method" are not going to detect the divine Creator and his project. It isn't that they lack evidence supporting intelligent design but, rather, that their allegedly scientific method is flawed. Certainly, if we presuppose that God does not exist, the theory of evolution becomes more attractive because it's all we have left. But that doesn't make it *true*. Darwinian evolution may be the best *naturalistic* explanation, but we are looking for the best explanation *period*.

The starting point and information

We should note that Darwin's theory of evolution doesn't explain much about the "origin of living beings." Natural selection *presupposes* that a living being already exists, with one or more completely functioning cells, ready to reproduce and susceptible to random mutation. That's asking a lot from square one. The theory doesn't even attempt to explain how matter came to be (we'll talk about that in the next chapter), or how *life itself* began. It doesn't explain how the first living, self-reproducing cell came into existence.

This starting point may have seemed unimportant during Darwin's lifetime, but we have since discovered that even a cell is *full* of incredibly complex mechanisms, like something out of an engineering laboratory. Cells contain an entire factory, including assembly lines, control mechanisms, trains to transport elements from one place to another so they can be utilized, energy management systems, and the DNA computer language that codes instructions to synthesize proteins. All of this exists on a microscopic scale.

Just to understand what is going on inside a cell, we need advanced knowledge of mechanical engineering. So when Albert Jacquard writes that "the mystery of life was reduced to the trivial game of elemental forces at the heart of the DNA molecule,"[21] I'd like to know what he means by "trivial."

Jacques Monod, on the other hand, understands that, without a creator, the discovery of the genetic code at the cellular level presents a serious challenge to naturalism:

> The major problem is the origin of the genetic code and of its translation mechanism. Indeed, instead of a problem it ought rather to be called a riddle.
>
> The code is meaningless unless translated. The modern cell's translating machinery consists of at least fifty macromolecular components *which are themselves coded in DNA: the code cannot be translated otherwise than by products of translation.*[22]

Did you catch that? All these mechanisms had to be in place *before* any mutations or natural selection could even begin, and Darwinian evolution doesn't even attempt to explain how they appeared in the first place. The only thing the theory tries to explain is how the species became more complex and diversified, starting with an ancestor we presume to have existed. But I contend that even this limited amount of explanation is open to doubt.

A gigantic extrapolation

We don't have room here for an in-depth discussion of the multitude of biological arguments proposed on both sides of the debate, but I can at least speak to what is at stake in these discussions.

If the theory of Darwinian evolution is true, the action took place in a very distant past and at an extremely slow rate. Thus, it is impossible to claim that we can reproduce the same circumstances that would allow us to observe the random mutations of different species and see their evolution in real time.

In the best-case studies, it is possible to simulate a kind of accelerated Darwinian process by doing artificial selection in a lab and directing the reproduction of individual members of a species. Then, by observing these minor mutations, scientists can *extrapolate* the data to determine whether these same processes could have occurred in nature, without outside "intelligent" intervention, to produce all the species from all times on the entire earth over millions of years.

Is this gigantic extrapolation truly justified? That is the question that skeptics of Darwinian evolution have posed. The only things we can observe in nature, and even in the laboratory, are minor reversible variations that are often destructive to the existing species rather than beneficial to their survival.

It is extremely difficult for random mutation to produce any kind of advantageous morphological change that could begin to explain the transition from one species to another. Quite the opposite. Instead of producing new and useful functions, the vast majority of genetic mutations *destroy* existing functionality. And it isn't difficult to see why. Imagine the effects of random changes to the words of a novel, or the binary code of a piece of software. Without a novelist or a software engineer, the results would be catastrophic. Jean-Paul Sartre's *Being and Nothingness* will not transform itself into *Les Misérables*, and Microsoft Windows won't morph into Mac OS through random selection.

Let's consider the similarly complex proposition that whales (the largest mammal) evolved, through the mechanism of random mutation, from an ancestor who once lived entirely on land. How do we transform a terrestrial animal into one that lives its life underwater? In the same way we would transform a car into a submarine! It's a massive undertaking.[23] Changing one into the other would require countless intentional and coordinated changes. In the case of the whale, hundreds of thousands of morphological changes would be necessary, and it has never been proved that Darwinian evolution is able to do that, especially in the amount of time allowed.

The Darwinians themselves estimate that our planet is only 4.5 billion years old. On top of that, the vast majority of species have developed in only the past 600 million years. This period corresponds to what researchers call the "Cambrian explosion." In fossil excavations, we don't see the slow and gradual emergence of species changing little by little from beginning to end. On the contrary, we observe a multitude of families of species that appear "overnight" on a cosmic scale, during the Cambrian explosion. Under these conditions, it is very difficult to justify the enormous Darwinian extrapolation, which claims that random mutations filtered by natural selection produced all the species that ever existed in this limited time frame.

So is it *possible*, despite these counterarguments, that a Darwinian mechanism might have won the lottery and produced all of the species from all of history in the allotted time frame? It is difficult to prove that it could not be so. However, one thing seems clear: In the light of scientific evidence, it would not be irrational to find this theory highly improbable.

Christians are not the only ones who doubt this theory. Francis Crick himself proposed and defended a theory called "directed panspermia," which suggests that life did *not* begin on Earth but was transplanted from somewhere else in space. Very well. This position seems to at least recognize that there was not enough time on Earth for all these changes. I agree with him there. I simply find the God hypothesis is preferable to that of extraterrestrials.

To conclude, the Darwinian theory of evolution doesn't offer much in the way of refuting theism. Christians may reasonably reconcile the two theories or simply reject Darwinian evolution. Even though the second option tends to draw mockery, neither position equates to intellectual suicide.

The Gould standard

In order to have intelligent conversations when corresponding with my friends, I bought a few DVDs of scientific documentaries and watched them alone in my apartment. Then my friend Frank, who studied biology and was also a reader of the Jesus newsletters, recommended I read a book by a famous evolutionary scientist named Stephen Jay Gould.

I recognized the author's name because my atheist godmother had already talked to me about him in an email. She had told me it was unreasonable to reject evolution today after reading Gould.

Since his name had come up twice in the form of an objection, I decided to buy Gould's book *Hen's Teeth and Horse's Toes*. This was probably the first time I had bought a serious book without being forced to by a professor. The idea of sitting down and reading an entire book seemed strange to me, especially since the table of contents didn't look entirely relevant. So I just read the section where Gould defends evolution.

To my great surprise, the only examples he gave were the peppered moth mutations and Ernst Haeckel's embryo drawings—two hot-button illustrations commonly debated in online forums with a lot of finger-pointing and accusations of intellectual dishonesty on both sides of the issue. Not very helpful. In fairness, Gould's book was more than twenty-five years old at the time I picked it up and was admittedly outdated. I mentioned this in one of my newsletters, and my readers were quick to agree that the material was no longer pertinent. We went on to discuss other subjects.

When I thought about it, I found I really enjoyed the discussions and the debates that arose from my Jesus newsletters, and it was gratifying to be able to calmly answer my friends' objections. My knowledge was still very limited, but with a bit of research and logical thinking, I was able to rationally defend my ideas.

One day, a friend called to invite me to a conference at her church. She said it was on "Christian apologetics." I hadn't heard that term before.

"Thanks for the invitation," I replied, "but what is it? Why do you think I would like this conference?"

"Apologetics is the rational defense of the Christian faith. They'll be asking the kinds of intellectual questions on the truth of Christianity that interest you. The conference is going to be on different worldviews and how to determine their veracity. I really think you should come."

"Okay, I guess I'll come and see."

11

Discovering Apologetics

• • •

Of all studies most brutalizing, most destructive
of all poetry, theology is the first.

ERNEST RENAN

BY THE TIME THE CONFERENCE was scheduled to begin, the
auditorium was filled to capacity. The event was held in a
church, but there were no songs and no sermon. The speaker
simply walked over to the podium and began his presentation. I listened intently as he explained the art of rationally
defending the truth of the Christian faith, and it occurred to
me that "apologetics" was more or less what I had naturally
started doing with my Jesus newsletters.

The speaker gave us some tests to evaluate the truth of
our own worldviews, and he discussed God's existence as it
related to the beginning of the universe, the basis of morality, the meaning of life, and the possibility of life after death.

I was intrigued. It was my first formal encounter with the discipline of apologetics, and I was hooked. I felt an inner desire, almost an itch—what some people might describe as a calling.

So this is what I'm supposed to be doing . . .

I had gone to the event with Pastor Vinny, and afterward he turned to me with a big smile and said, "So, Guillaume, what did you think?"

When I told him my reaction, he encouraged me to "scratch the itch." I went home that night absorbed in thought, and yet slept like a rock.

Strange diet

The next morning, I went online and ordered a book on Christian apologetics and a set of DVDs containing some recorded lectures. Soon I was ordering even more books by various Christian apologists. Before long, I went from almost never reading a book apart from school to a point where it seemed I couldn't stop reading. As soon as I left the office each night, I would rush home, grab a slice or two of New York style pizza from a place around the corner from my building so I wouldn't waste time cooking, and then spend the entire evening reading books and watching documentaries, Q&A sessions, and academic debates on DVD.

I basically had no social life at the time, I wasn't playing volleyball or music, I didn't have a girlfriend, and my family was thousands of miles away. I was free to give undivided attention to my research, and my excitement increased as I absorbed the material.

After a few weeks of this regimen, and of eating poorly, my tongue started tingling. My terrible diet had resulted in the first stages of scurvy. I quickly solved the problem with large doses of orange juice and decided to begin eating more healthily. However, my diet of relentless study continued. Logic, history, science, philosophy, and anything pertaining to Christianity became a part of my research.

One of the DVDs contained a discussion on the subject of morality between an atheist, a Hindu, and two Christian apologists. The conversation was interesting in and of itself, but what really caught my attention was one of the two Christians on the platform, whom I had not seen before. He was a bearded man, short of stature, sitting discreetly off to one side. He didn't call attention to himself at first, but as soon as he was given the floor, the weight of his arguments and the clarity of his explanations took me by surprise. What intellectual power! I immediately picked up the DVD case to look for his name: William Lane Craig.

All right, Mr. Craig, let's see if you have anything to sell on the internet.

A quick online search uncovered a two-hour-plus video, titled "Atheism vs. Christianity," in which Craig debates an atheist scholar named Frank Zindler. I watched it immediately. Craig's performance was epic. He offered arguments that were logical, powerful, and understandable, and he refuted his atheist opponent's arguments with amazing eloquence.

I quickly learned that Craig was a philosopher and an expert on the existence of God and the resurrection of Jesus. He had earned two doctorates, one in philosophy and the other in theology. If debating on God's existence were a sport, William Lane Craig would be the world champion. His debate against Frank Zindler was a crushing defeat for Zindler.

Once I finished watching the debate, I ordered Craig's signature book, *Reasonable Faith*, and another book, titled *Does God Exist?*, which is a transcription of a debate that Craig had with Antony Flew, the most well-known atheist philosopher of the past century. I devoured both of them.

Cause and Effect

William Lane Craig is generally known for his debates on the existence of God. But as I read about his work and his interactions with atheist philosophers, I discovered he was especially appreciated in academic circles for another feat: his masterful defense of a philosophical and scientific argument for the existence of God known as the "kalam cosmological argument."[1] Craig's writings on the subject triggered so many discussions that it's probably the most talked about argument for the existence of God in the philosophical literature today.

At the apologetics conference I had attended, it had been mentioned that the beginning of the universe raised the question of a creator; but now I discovered that William Lane Craig offered a logical and rigorous formulation of the argument:

- Whatever begins to exist has a cause.

- The universe began to exist.

- Therefore, the universe had a cause.

Then, by simply analyzing what the cause of the universe must be, Craig shows that it has a number of particularly relevant properties. For example, the cause of the universe must be beyond space and time, which means it must be immaterial, spaceless, timeless (and thus, eternal), and incredibly powerful, since it was able to create the entire universe. It must also be personal because only two types of objects can be immaterial:

1. Abstract objects (such as numbers or propositions). But abstract objects cannot be the cause of anything, much less the cause of the universe.
2. An immaterial soul: a person (without a body). This is exactly what Christians claim to be true of God.

This argument brings us back not only to the cause of the universe but also to its transcendent and personal creator, whom the Bible says created the heavens and the earth "in the beginning."[2]

But what do the skeptics say about it?

Bertrand Russell denies *both* premises. "There is no reason why the world could not have come into being without a cause; nor, on the other hand, is there any reason why it should not have always existed."[3]

Russell insists that the universe could have begun without a cause. But this is not reasonable. There is a highly intuitive and universally verified principle of metaphysics which says that nothing comes out of nothing. Voltaire admits it: "No axiom has ever been more universally received than this: 'Of nothing, nothing comes.' Indeed, the contrary is incomprehensible."[4] And if this principle is faulty, why would only universes spring up out of nothing? Why wouldn't we see croissants, philosophers, or tropical islands appear out of nothing before our very eyes? Even Baron d'Holbach is forced to agree that "nothing can be made of nothing."[5] This premise seems clear for the reasonable skeptic. But then we must ask the question: Did the universe actually have a beginning?

Baron d'Holbach doesn't think so. On the contrary, he affirms that the universe "is of itself that which it is; it exists necessarily and from all eternity."[6] Prosper Alfaric suggests that the world "exists in and of itself" and that matter "had no more of a beginning than it will an ending."[7]

As for Michel Onfray, he accuses Christians of being opposed to science, mentioning "the eternity of the universe" in a list of scientific theses rejected by believers: "Is there anything to be said for scientific belief in the eternity of the universe? In multiple universes? (Both Epicurean theses, incidentally . . .) Absolutely not! God created the universe from nothing. Before nothing, there was . . . nothing."[8]

I'm not sure who Onfray is thinking of when he tells us that scientists believe in the eternity of the universe because modern science teaches exactly the opposite. The vast majority of scientific evidence points to a beginning of the universe. The standard model is the Big Bang theory, which places the absolute beginning of space and time around 13.7 billion years ago.[9] Albert Jacquard explains the consequences of this model:

> Since the Big Bang has been defined as both the beginning of space and of the objects contained therein, it is also of necessity the beginning of time, which only began to tick away from that moment on. There was therefore no "before."[10]

There are many good reasons besides this one to affirm a beginning. Some are scientific (the expansion of the universe, the cosmic microwave background, the second law of thermodynamics), and others are philosophical (the impossibility of having an actually infinite set of moments in the past or the impossibility of crossing over an infinite past to arrive at today). These reasons are convincing, but for a complete defense, I invite you to take a more in-depth look at the philosophical and scientific literature that deals with each of them. For our purposes here, I'll simply say that the beginning of the universe is at least the standard scientific model, and that when Michel Onfray affirms "the eternity of the universe," he is the one turning his back on modern science while accusing Christians of living in the Dark Ages.

There are also some atheist objections based on a lack of understanding of the argument. Bertrand Russell quips, "If everything must have a cause, then God must have a cause. If there can be anything without a cause, it may just as well be the world as God, so that there cannot be any validity in that argument."[11]

This proves a lack of understanding of the first premise of the argument. The believer does not claim that *everything* must have a cause but only *"that which begins to exist."* Since God exists outside of time, he does not have a beginning and, hence, he has no need of a cause.

Why couldn't that be the case with the universe? *Because it has a beginning!*

Prosper Alfaric misrepresents the first premise when he says that "all beings, and all movement in general, comes from another and that one from another still."[12] But that is not what the argument says. All beings *which begin to exist* must "come from another." These critics are not interacting with the theist's true argument; they are missing the mark.

Jean Meslier asks how God could have caused the universe without preceding it in time: "If time was something that could be created and even if it were created, as our 'God-lovers' would have us believe, it certainly could only have been created by a being that preceded it, because if this being did not precede it, how could he have created it?"[13]

The answer is simple: God precedes the universe *logically* but not *temporally*. There is no reason to think it was impossible for God, who exists outside of time, to freely create the universe before time existed. If it seems strange to the atheist that the universe was created without a temporal cause, the atheist scenario is stranger still because there is no cause, either inside or outside of time.

So the *kalam* cosmological argument holds up quite well before its critics, and it supports the existence of a God who created the universe.

Fine-tuned

In William Lane Craig's writings, I found another similar argument supporting the existence of God. If you aren't passionate about cosmology and astrophysics—why not?— I can't necessarily blame you, but I invite you to hang in there because I can (and therefore, I will) present this final argument quite succinctly. It is one of the most powerful arguments in favor of the existence of a Creator, and it's called the "fine-tuning argument."

Modern science has discovered a certain number of constants intervening in the equations of the fundamental laws of physics (e.g., the gravitational constant, the mass ratio between electrons and protons, the charge of electrons), as well as a certain number of initial quantities in the universe (e.g., expansion speed, the level of initial entropy) that seem to have been adjusted to an immeasurable precision in order to allow life in the universe. If these constants or quantities were even a fraction smaller or greater, life would be impossible anywhere in the universe.

How do we explain this remarkable fact? Is it simply random chance that life can be sustained in our universe? Most likely not. The numbers are such that it would have been billions and billions of times more probable that we'd end up with a universe which doesn't permit any life forms. Is it due to physical necessity? Probably not since variations in these constants and quantities would have been compatible with our same laws of nature; there is no reason to believe that this fine-tuning is physically necessary. Therefore, we have only one plausible alternative explanation: The universe displays fine-tuning in order to support life because the universe was finely tuned to support life. Once again, this implies that there is a creator and a designer behind the universe, who finely tuned it to allow the existence of life.

So what do the skeptics say about that?

As I mentioned before, Michel Onfray criticizes Christians for rejecting certain scientific theses, among these the theory of "multiple universes." This theory is also known as the "multiverse theory." I will add here that Christians don't necessarily need to reject this theory because it is entirely compatible with God's existence. But what exactly does this theory propose?

The multiverse theory claims that there is a multitude, or even an infinity, of parallel universes beyond our own. Each has its own constants and differing values in the equations that govern its laws of physics. The multiverse theory is often proposed as an answer to the fine-tuning argument. It's a way to rescue the hypothesis of chance. To wit, if there exists an infinite number of parallel universes with differing values, it raises the probability that one of them would randomly hit on the right numbers to support life.

However, two problems make this theory unattractive. First, there is no conclusive and independent evidence in favor of the multiverse. So far, no one has made contact with any of these other parallel universes. This is not prohibitive in and of itself because the absence of proof is not necessarily proof of absence. But if the only reason the multiverse theory is adopted is to avoid the conclusion that our universe has a designer, then it's not very satisfying. It's more akin to presupposing that God does not exist, rather than an example of following the scientific evidence wherever it leads.

Second, and more important, if our universe is only one in an infinite series, it is extremely improbable that it would be as *big* as it is. Among the set of possible universes that would allow life, the probability of having a universe much smaller than ours is extremely high. So the size of our universe undermines the hypothesis of chance. The multiverse theory is not a good answer to the fine-tuning argument.

As for André Comte-Sponville, he distorts the argument's affirmations:

You start out by observing the world; you note that there is order in the world, order of daunting complexity; and you conclude that there must be an ordering intelligence. This is what, today, is known as the theory of intelligent design. The world, it claims, is too well ordered, too complex, too beautiful, too harmonious to be the result of mere chance; at the origin of such extraordinary beauty and complexity there can only be a creative, ordering intelligence, which must be God.[14]

I find at least two errors in Comte-Sponville's presentation of the argument. First, it is not mere complexity that supports the conclusion of "intelligent design"; it is *specified* complexity, a complexity *that has an objective* and that corresponds to an independent pattern.

Let me explain.

Every mountain in nature displays very complex rock patterns, but that doesn't lead us to a conclusion of intelligent design. Mount Rushmore, on the other hand, with the faces of four former presidents carved into the rock, corresponds to an independent pattern—namely the portraits of the presidents—which allows us to conclude that it is the product of intelligent design. It is this *specified* complexity that leads us to infer the presence of intelligent design.

In the same way, the improbability of the combination of constants and initial quantities in our universe does not, in and of itself, lead us to infer the presence of intelligent design; but the fact that this combination occurred precisely in the tiny window of possibility that would allow life in the universe leads us to believe in a design by the Creator of the universe. And no one says that an intelligent design with God as the Author is the *only* possible explanation. But it is by far the better explanation. It is an inference to the best explanation, which I think is quite justified.

Comte-Sponville submits another objection, that of "imperfections," as he criticizes the well-known design argument given by William Paley. In his famous "watchmaker" analogy, Paley said that if he were walking along in the countryside and stumbled upon a watch lying by the roadside, it would be logical to infer that an intelligent designer created the watch and its complex mechanisms that allow us to measure time. In *The Little Book of Atheist Spirituality*, Comte-Sponville criticizes this analogy.

> It makes short shrift of the countless examples of
> *disorder*, horror and dysfunction in the universe.
> A cancerous tumor can also be described as a kind
> of clock (as in a time bomb); an earthquake, if we
> wish to prolong the clockwork metaphor, would be
> something like a planetary buzzer or alarm. Does this
> prove that tumors and cataclysms are all part of an
> intelligent, benevolent design?[15]

This objection is poorly formulated. We're not claiming we can use the fine-tuning argument to prove that the intelligent creator is also omniscient and benevolent. That isn't the purpose of the argument. And even if the design were evil and imperfect (which it is not—the Christian view of Creation is that a good design was subsequently spoiled by sin), the fact that there *is* a design still implies the existence of an intelligent creator. An imperfect design is still an intelligent design, and an evil design is still an intelligent design. A Yugo was the fruit of intelligent design even though it wasn't a BMW; and a torture rack is the fruit of intelligent design even though it wasn't a massage table.

In any case, the problem of imperfections, or of evil, is irrelevant to the fine-tuning argument, which powerfully supports the existence of an intelligent creator. In fact, Antony Flew, the famous atheist philosopher whose debate with William Lane Craig was part of my reading, later changed his mind and renounced atheism, in large part due to the fine-tuning argument.

While I'm at it . . .

My nightly study routine went on for months. Little by little, and with each book I read, I discovered new authors, often in the footnotes of the current book I was reading. I learned about these authors, bought their books, watched their debates, and studied all the relevant material on the subject.

After months of repeating this same routine, I started thinking, *If I'm going to spend all my time and my resources studying this stuff, I might as well get a degree in it.* So I applied to the master's program at Alliance Theological

Seminary, part of Nyack College in Manhattan. Because I still had my day job, I was happy to learn that the university offered evening classes. I hired a translation company that specializes in transposing school transcripts from one country to another to get a copy of my grades in English. I hoped that my excellent results in engineering school would make up for the fact that I didn't have any formal theological training. I soon received a letter informing me that I had been admitted as a student at the theological seminary.

For my first semester, wanting to jump right into the heart of the academic side of things, I chose two systematic theology classes. On the evening of my first class, not knowing what to expect, I headed over to campus.

Would I even understand what they were talking about? As a Christian recently converted from atheism, would I be able to fly under the radar and blend in with the other students, who had probably all been Christians from childhood? Would I fail completely? I wasn't sure of anything.

The systematic theology professor introduced himself and told us that the class would be on "the attributes of God." Then he said, "Before we begin talking about God's attributes, we need to ask ourselves, 'Does God even exist?'" He proceeded to go through all the classic arguments in favor of God's existence.

Wow, what a stroke of luck! I thought. *With all my study of apologetics, I already know this all by heart.* The professor even used some of William Lane Craig's work.

He quickly saw that I had a good understanding of the subject, and he invited me to answer some of the more technical objections brought up by another student. What a satisfying surprise!

When the class session was over, I walked to the train station, filled with a deep sense of joy. I couldn't help smiling from ear to ear because I felt I was doing what God wanted me to do. I felt like I was right where he wanted me. I was moving forward in the right direction.

My other classes went just as well. Apparently, my private, personal research had really prepared me for them. I continued to learn—reading, writing papers, and enjoying the discussion times. Three years later, I completed my master's degree in biblical literature, with an emphasis on the New Testament, with "honors and distinction." I even got to experience an American graduation ceremony—complete with a black robe, colorful regalia, and a mortarboard. Just like in the movies.

In my free time—between going to class and working on Wall Street—I embarked on a slightly crazy personal project as well: writing a book. I had an excellent professor during my second semester at the university, and he and I struck up a friendship. Louis DeCaro Jr. teaches biblical theology, Christian history, and hermeneutics (the study of methods of interpretation). His mastery of the Bible fascinated me, and I loved discovering deep truths about Jesus during his classes.

One day, before class began, Professor DeCaro handed me a paper I had written on man's free will in relation to

God's sovereignty (a classic subject in the theological and philosophical literature). He said something that really surprised me: "Guillaume, your arguments are interesting and original. Have you ever thought about publishing them in a book?"

"Ummm . . . no, never," I replied.

He suggested I give it a try. I felt it was a bit beyond me, but I decided to listen to him and see what I could do. I began writing down ideas, and I bought some books on the subject to test my theories. I ended up interacting with dozens of books written by experts on the subject. By the time my master's program was over, I had a very imperfect rough draft of an entire book on the subject of free will, and the topic was beginning to fascinate me. I wasn't sure what to do with my manuscript, so I put it on the back burner for a while.

Doctorate

One year after I completed my master's, I went back to the same seminary to take advantage of the one free class every student was allowed to audit after earning a degree there. I decided to take a class on the book of Revelation with Professor Glen Shellrude, who taught classes in the New Testament, ancient Greek, and first-century Greco-Roman civilization. Professors DeCaro and Shellrude were my two favorite instructors during my time in seminary, and we remained friends after I graduated. By then, I was calling them Lou and Glen. Glen was thrilled to see me back in one of his classes, and now it was his turn to play a decisive role in my future.

One day, after class, he asked me, "Guillaume, when are you going to start work on your doctorate?"

I had entertained the idea of a PhD in the past, but I wasn't sure it was right for me. Normally, one would pursue a doctorate in order to become an expert on a professional level and eventually teach at a university. Was that really what I wanted to do? And would it even be possible, considering I also had a full-time job on Wall Street? I couldn't quit my job because by that time I had a wife and a baby on the way. On top of that, if I wanted to earn a doctorate in the United States, I would have to complete two years of full-time study and pass the comprehensive exams before I could even begin writing my thesis.

But Glen had a better idea. He explained that doctoral programs in the United Kingdom weren't set up in the same way as in the US. In Britain, I would conduct academic research, mostly on my own, and then would defend my thesis. And most of the work could be done at a distance, so I would not have to relocate in order to join the program.

Glen put me in contact with a Cambridge scholar, who put me in touch with a philosopher in Liverpool, who, in turn, gave me the contact information for another British philosopher, Paul Helm, who was well-known to me, at least from his work. I had discovered Helm's writings while I was researching free will. He was a recognized expert on the subject and a respected practitioner of the discipline. Though no longer teaching college classes, he still supervised doctoral theses at a university near London.[16] What an incredible opportunity!

I sent in my application form and quickly found myself in a video conference with Professor Helm and the university's director of studies. They asked me what I wanted to write my thesis on, and it wasn't hard for me to come up with an answer: the metaphysics of free will. I already had the rough draft of my book on the same subject, filled with original material that could be applied to my doctoral thesis. Paul Helm was more than happy to supervise my thesis on the subject, and I was accepted.

I began my long-distance research from New York. My wife, Katherine, had warned me in the past: "If you ever want to pursue a doctorate, it would be good to have it done before we have children." Of course, she had been right, except that our daughter was born a month *before* the program started. So much for wisdom. I learned to write my thesis on the computer with one hand while holding a baby in the other, and I changed her diapers between reading articles on analytical philosophy.

It was Katherine's devotion to our family that allowed me to balance everything. She took excellent care of our daughter even though she was still finishing her *own* studies. We learned to multitask. I woke up very early every morning and worked on my research before heading out to my job on the trading floor so I could spend my evenings and weekends with my wife and daughter.

Reading, writing, reading, writing, little by little, I wrote my thesis. The process went on for several months, which then turned into years. In the meantime, I joined several professional philosophical and theological societies and presented my work at their conferences.

Over the next two years, we added two adorable little boys to our family, which means we had three children under the age of three! Despite all this, I finally managed to submit my thesis. I flew over to London for the oral defense, and my performance convinced the examiners to grant me my doctorate in philosophy—the same subject in which I had received a failing grade in my high school finals.

So where am I headed now? Only God knows for sure. I still work as a software engineering manager, and my academic studies have continued as well. I have written a few books and articles, taught philosophy as an adjunct professor at the university, and been invited to speak at conferences and on college campuses.

So that's how God took this atheistic, hedonistic software engineer who scorned religion, grabbed him by the scruff of the neck, demolished his intellectual objections, changed his heart, forgave his sins, and made him into a philosopher, theologian, and apologist of the Christian faith.

Now before I conclude, let me tell the story of how I met my wife and explain some of my motivation for writing this book.

My Motivation
for Writing

● ● ●

He who finds a wife finds a good thing
and obtains favor from the LORD.

PROVERBS 18:22

THE STORY OF HOW MY ENTIRE ADULT LIFE was turned upside-down by God would obviously not be complete if I didn't tell you the story of how I met my wife. It all began when I met a marvelous and beautiful young woman who was on a yearlong sabbatical in Paris before beginning her graduate studies in America.

Not long before I started at the seminary in New York, I went home to Paris for a week to see my family. On Sunday morning, I went to the service at Robert's church, hoping to catch up with him afterward. Over the years, and with all the time we'd spent together leading up to my conversion, we had become good friends. I was looking forward to hearing Robert preach, and I hoped we could maybe have lunch together.

I sat off to the right in the sanctuary, not far from where I had sat during my first visit to the church, all those years ago, when I was still an atheist. We began to sing, and I tried to focus on the words, but my eyes kept wandering over to a young woman with light hair sitting to my left in the first row. I hadn't seen her before, and I assumed she had joined the church after I left for New York. Finally, when the sermon began, I was able to tear my eyes away and concentrate on the message.

After the service, Robert and his family came over to greet me.

"Guillaume, I'm very sorry, but I'm not free for lunch today," Robert said. "But let's try to get together one day this week, okay?"

"Yes, I would like that," I said.

Robert gestured to the others who were standing with him, and said, "You already know Kathryn and my girls, Rachelle and Réanna, but I'd like to introduce you to Elizabeth, our assistant and au pair."

It was her—the charming young woman from the first row! She was even more beautiful up close, and her face was radiant. She had sparkling brown eyes, slightly rosy cheeks, and a smile to die for. She said hello in French with the most adorable American accent.

"I'm making lunch for the girls today," she said, "but there's enough for everyone. Would you like to eat with us?"

She didn't have to twist my arm.

"Of course, I'd love to eat with you."

Over lunch, I learned that Elizabeth had come to spend a year with Robert's family, take care of the girls, and work at the church as Robert and Kathryn's assistant before beginning a graduate program in art at Virginia Commonwealth University.

The more we talked, the more I thought, *This woman is absolutely amazing.* She was a fashion designer and also a painter, photographer, dancer, singer, pianist, and guitarist—and she spoke fluent French. The eldest of six children, she had grown up in Virginia, but her parents were from Alaska, and she had spent her summers there, exploring nature surrounded by bears, moose, whales, orcas, and bald eagles. Her grandfather had a fishing boat, and she often went along with him as he fished for salmon, halibut, and crab off the Alaskan coast. She had traveled widely during her year in Europe, and she knew Paris better than I did.

Because Robert hadn't been available on Sunday, he invited me over for lunch the following day. I was happy to see him, of course, but I was also curious to see whether the au pair would be present. Sure enough, Elizabeth was there, and she had made chocolate chip cookies, which alone would have won me over if I hadn't already been smitten.

Robert and I chatted in his office for several hours, and then I had a few minutes to talk to Elizabeth in the living room. I loved every minute with her, and I began to think about how we might see each other again.

I knew it was improbable because I was going back to New York and she would return to Virginia when her sabbatical year was up. It would have been awkward for me to suggest that I drive all the way down from New York to Virginia to see her, meet her family, and "go out for coffee and see what comes of it." At the very least, we needed to be "together" officially, and I knew that wouldn't happen before I left for New York.

I told her we should keep in touch, and we exchanged addresses and phone numbers. When I glanced at the card, I was surprised to see that she had written her name as "Katherine Jones."

What? I thought her name was Elizabeth.

It turned out that because Robert's wife's name was Kathryn, they had all agreed to call Katherine by her middle name, Elizabeth, while she was staying at their house, to avoid unnecessary confusion—for themselves, at least!

I went back to New York, and we started corresponding. I still didn't see how a romantic relationship could come of it, but I prayed, *Lord, I really like her, but all the doors seem closed for now. If you think that things could work between us and that we'd make a good couple, please open the door. Make a way for us to see each other again.*

A few weeks later, my boss called me into his office.

"Guillaume, I'm sorry. I know you just got back from vacation in France, but I need to send you to Paris on a business trip. Is that okay?"

Incredible.

I wrote to Katherine, "I'm coming back to Paris in three weeks. Do you want to get together?"

She said yes, and we went out on our first date. We had dinner in Paris, at the restaurant of the four-star hotel where my company put me up. After dinner, we went out for a romantic stroll in the gardens around the Louvre, to see the sunset and the Eiffel Tower sparkling in the night. At the end of the evening, I walked her back to her train, and we were officially "together."

Katherine completed her year of university studies in Virginia, and we maintained our long-distance relationship. I promised to wait for her, even if her studies kept us separated for four years. But the summer after her first year, she found out she could transfer to one of the best fashion schools in the country, the famous Fashion Institute of Technology (FIT), which is located in New York.

She handed in her application file, accompanied by an artistic portfolio, and we waited to hear. Despite the fact that FIT accepted only a handful of students each year, I was sure she would be one of them. So I made the bold move and surprised her by asking her to marry me. She, of course, said yes (or I wouldn't be telling this story), her acceptance letter arrived from FIT on the heels of my proposal, and she moved to New York.

The following summer, we were married in Virginia, in a big American wedding with all the trimmings, with friends and family from New York, Virginia, Alaska, and France. And two years after we had first met, we exchanged our very first kiss when the pastor said, "You may kiss the bride."

Fifteen years later

A little more than fifteen years have passed since my conversion, and my life is very different from what I would have imagined in my younger years. It's also much more beautiful than I could have dreamed. My wife is amazing, and we're having a wonderful time raising five adorable kids together. Plus, I have an interesting job that allows me to provide for my family.

I don't play volleyball anymore. I tried to defend my country's colors on the beach volleyball courts in Central Park a few times, and I even pulled off a few impressive spikes, but my shoulder still bothered me. My doctors finally found out what was wrong: One of the muscles that keeps the shoulder in place had completely atrophied. You can actually see an indentation in the muscles of my back, along my right shoulder blade. I wear it as sort of a badge of honor; a wound that God used to push me across the threshold of a Parisian church on a Sunday morning many years ago.

As for my musical career, I started playing keyboards again when I moved to New York, and I was even part of the worship band at my church for a while. But between work, studies, and writing projects, I didn't have much time to devote to it. Since then, Katherine and I have purchased a beautiful upright piano, and I'm passing the torch by teaching my daughter the basics.

Fifteen years later, I'm still friends with Robert, of

course. He's still a pastor in France, and we get together whenever my family vacations in Paris. Katherine designed his daughter Réanna's wedding dress, after completing her studies at FIT (with two babies in her arms) and after starting her own company designing wedding dresses and lingerie.

Pastor Vinny and I still get together from time to time, but not as often as I'd like because of our busy schedules. Every time we see each other, we pick right up where we left off, discussing theology as if we'd never been apart.

Thus far, no one in my family has placed their faith in Jesus. Of course, I love them all unconditionally—today more than ever. My big brother is still my hero, and in my mind, my little sister is still the little blonde, curly-haired sweetheart she always was. They are both married now and have given me an adorable passel of nieces and nephews.

My parents divorced not long after Katherine and I were married, and both have remarried. I love them with all my heart, and I'll never be able to repay them for all they've done. As you can imagine, they are crazy about their American grandchildren.

As for my commitment to God, I've had the privilege to answer his call on my life. Through my writing and conferences, I proclaim and defend the good news of Christ crucified and risen from the dead. Over the years, I've met and become friends with many of my heroes in the areas of philosophy, theology, and apologetics. It all seems a bit surreal sometimes.

One book, three goals

Before I end this book, I feel that I should say something about my motivation in writing it and possibly anticipate a potential objection.

Why did I write this book? Did I have an ulterior motive? Maybe even a hidden agenda? Is it a barely masked attempt at *proselytizing*? This frightening word is often used when someone recommends a religious belief to another person. So what do I have to say for myself?

I've chosen my dear Baron d'Holbach to defend me.

No man writes with a design to injure his fellow-creatures; he always proposes to himself to merit their suffrages, either by amusing them, by exciting their curiosity, or by communicating to them discoveries which he believes useful.[1]

I hope to have accomplished all three objectives. I hope I've amused you with my story, excited your curiosity by my apologetics, and communicated a "discovery which I believe useful" by my proclamation of the gospel. This book is obviously not just a memoir; it's also an invitation to follow me in this adventure. If the gospel of Jesus Christ is true, it's true for everyone. If my salvation and eternal life were freely granted by faith in Jesus, as the Bible says, then both are freely available to you as well.

Though I now believe in these things, having found life in

Jesus, I can't (and don't want to) force anyone else to believe them. But I think I must at least proclaim the message to anyone who wants to hear it. In so doing, I joyfully obey Ernest Renan, who invites us all, almost impatiently: "In Heaven's name, if you do happen to have got hold of the truth, do address yourself to the whole of humanity."[2]

Sir, yes, sir!

The head and the heart

Becoming a Christian means a radical change. It entails a change of opinion, yes, but also a change of heart. It is at once a new intellectual belief and an emotional renewal. Some Christians, wanting to defend the intellectual merits of their faith, have tended to describe conversion as a purely intellectual process. For example, certain well-intentioned Christians, after discovering my story, have promoted it thusly: "A French atheist engineer studies the proofs of Christianity and becomes a Christian."

That's all true, but it isn't (and wasn't) that simple. Rational arguments are useful to help the mind understand and embrace the Christian faith, but accepting the gospel is not just an intellectual process. It involves repentance, a change of heart, for any person who will turn away from sin and place their faith in Christ. True conversion inevitably engages the emotions as well.

You've just read it for yourself: My conversion involved intellectual reflection, it's true; but it also clearly contained some very strong emotions. And that's how it should be! Someone who only believes intellectually in the truth of the existence of God and the resurrection of Jesus is not really a Christian. The Bible says that "even the demons *believe*" that God exists, and they "shudder."[3] The gospel doesn't invite us to merely *believe* in these truths on an intellectual level. It also asks us to repent of our sins and place our faith in Jesus. It is a *union* with the risen Christ, and this union necessarily involves our emotions.

Several years ago, as I was looking through some old books in my grandfather's library, one of the volumes caught my attention. It was apparently written by a Christian author. On the back cover, the sales copy proudly stated, "Finally, a well thought out conversion, devoid of emotions." In my opinion, that's like someone at a wedding writing in the guest book: "Finally, a wedding without emotions."

No, thank you.

I find the idea of a wedding to be a very fitting metaphor for conversion. When I married Katherine, I had many intellectual reasons to believe she would be an excellent wife and that this wedding was a good idea. But more importantly, I *loved her with all my heart*!

In a similar manner, it is a joyful event when a sinner is reconciled with God. Jesus often used parables to describe this. He said that God rejoices like a shepherd who finds a lost sheep and calls his friends to celebrate with him.[4] He likens God to a woman who searches high and low and finally finds a gold coin that she lost. She, too, calls her friends and neighbors to rejoice with her.[5] Or what about the parable of the prodigal son? The father runs to meet his son, offers him a ring, shoes, and a robe, and throws a party where he kills the fatted calf so that he and his loved ones can eat and rejoice together.[6]

On the other hand, Jesus speaks of sinners who find eternal life through the gospel. He compares them to a merchant seeking beautiful pearls, who, when he finds one, excitedly goes and sells everything he has in order to buy it.[7] He also compares them to a man who finds a treasure hidden in a field and joyfully sells everything he owns to buy the field.[8]

For someone who isn't used to it, the idea of rejoicing and "loving God" may sound a little bit strange. Why should we love him? How do we love him? We can't even see him!

Jesus gave us a wonderful example in a conversation he had with a Pharisee named Simon, who had invited him over for dinner.[9] While they were at the table, a woman came in to see Jesus. She was "a woman of the city, who was a sinner," probably a prostitute. She threw herself at Jesus' feet, crying. She wet his feet with her tears and covered them with perfume. When Simon the Pharisee saw what was happening, he said to himself that if Jesus were truly a prophet, he would know what kind of woman this was, and he wouldn't allow her to touch him.

Then Jesus told Simon a story.

"A certain moneylender had two debtors. One owed five hundred denarii, and the other fifty. When they could not pay, he cancelled the debt of both. Now which of them will love him more?"

Simon answered, "The one, I suppose, for whom he cancelled the larger debt."

Jesus said to him, "You have judged rightly."

Then he dealt the final blow:

"Do you see this woman? I entered your house; you gave me no water for my feet, but she has wet my feet with her tears and wiped them with her hair. You gave me no kiss, but from the time I came in she has not ceased to kiss my feet. You did not anoint my head with oil, but she has anointed my feet with ointment. Therefore I tell you, her sins, which are many, are forgiven—for she loved much. But he who is forgiven little, loves little."

When Jesus told the woman that her sins had been forgiven, the people seated around the table began to ask themselves: "Who is this, who even forgives sins?"

Then Jesus said to the woman, "Your faith has saved you; go in peace."

This illustration is powerful. Jesus speaks of loving God because God has forgiven our sins. He who is forgiven little, loves little, and he who is forgiven much, loves much.

I love much.

About the Author

• • •

GUILLAUME BIGNON is a French philosopher who was born and raised near Paris. He became passionate about Christian philosophy and apologetics after an unlikely and providential conversion from atheism to Christianity in his twenties. This led him to attend Alliance Theological Seminary in New York, where he obtained a master's in biblical literature, with an emphasis on the New Testament. His love for these topics drove him to continue his studies and complete a PhD in philosophical theology at the London School of Theology. Guillaume has had the opportunity to present lectures at meetings of the Evangelical Theological Society, the Evangelical Philosophical Society, and the Society of Christian Philosophers. His interests include the metaphysics of human free will as it relates to divine providence as well as natural theology and soteriology. Guillaume is an executive committee member of Association Axiome, a society of French-speaking Christian scholars. He currently works as a software engineering manager. He and his wife, Katherine, have five young (and adorable) children. Guillaume writes in English at thelogui.blogspot.com and in French at associationaxiome.com. Follow him on Twitter: @theoloGUI.

Notes

● ● ●

CHAPTER 2: A "MOST TENDER" CHILDHOOD

1. Matthew 4:1-11.
2. Baron d'Holbach, *Portable Theology*, trans. David Holohan (Kingston upon Thames, UK: Hodgson Press, 2010), 165.
3. d'Holbach, *Portable Theology*, 187.
4. Baron d'Holbach, *Le Christianisme dévoilé* [Christianity unveiled] (Londres: s.n., 1777), 58. Cited quote translated by Lori Varak.
5. Michel Onfray, *Atheist Manifesto* (New York: Arcade Publishing, 2007), 1.
6. Onfray, *Atheist Manifesto*, 2, 3.
7. Onfray, *Atheist Manifesto*, 3.
8. Onfray, *Atheist Manifesto*, 5, 92. Onfray attributes the terms "obsessional neurosis" and "hallucinatory psychosis" to Sigmund Freud in *The Future of an Illusion* (1927).
9. Onfray, *Atheist Manifesto*, 13.
10. Onfray, *Atheist Manifesto*, 35.
11. Ernest Renan, *The Future of Science* (Boston: Roberts Brothers, 1893), 296–297.
12. Luc Ferry goes so far as to say that "nearly 70% of French people today are still Christians." Luc Ferry, *Qu'est-ce qu'une vie réussie?* [What is a successful life?] (Paris: Grasset, 2002), 453. Cited quote translated by Lori Varak.
13. See, for example, Alvin Plantinga, *Warrant: The Current Debate* (Oxford: Oxford University Press, 1993), and Alvin Plantinga, *Warrant and Proper Function* (Oxford: Oxford University Press, 1993).
14. Charles Darwin, letter to William Graham, July 3, 1881, Darwin Correspondence Project, University of Cambridge, https://www.darwinproject.ac.uk/letter/?docId=letters/DCP-LETT-13230.xml;query=darwin;brand=default.

15. An atheist might respond: "If our cognitive faculties are trustworthy in discovering truth, it's obvious that they also give us an advantage as far as survival goes. Indeed, if I understand correctly the truth of the world around me, I am that much more apt to avoid dangers that would threaten my fragile life in hostile surroundings." The problem with this reasoning is that, in order to trust our cognitive faculties, instead of saying, "If they are trustworthy, they'll help us survive," we should say, "It is because they help us to survive that we consider them trustworthy." But this last statement is absolutely untrue. There is no reason to believe that if our cognitive faculties are adapted to survival, they are therefore trustworthy in producing true beliefs.

16. This so-called evolutionary argument against naturalism has notably been championed by Alvin Plantinga. See, for example, his *Where the Conflict Really Lies: Science, Religion, and Naturalism* (New York: Oxford University Press, 2011). Contemporary atheist philosopher Thomas Nagel reasons along the same lines: "Evolutionary naturalism implies that we shouldn't take any of our convictions seriously, including the scientific world picture on which evolutionary naturalism itself depends." Thomas Nagel, *Mind and Cosmos: Why the Materialist Neo-Darwinian Conception of Nature is Almost Certainly False* (New York: Oxford University Press, 2012), 28.

17. André Comte-Sponville, *The Little Book of Atheist Spirituality*, trans. Nancy Huston (New York: Viking, 2006), 82.

CHAPTER 3: RELENTLESS PURSUIT OF SUCCESS

1. Luc Ferry, *Man Made God: The Meaning of Life* (Chicago: University of Chicago Press, 2002), 9.

2. Sigmund Freud, quoted in Luc Ferry, *What Is the Good Life?*, trans. Lydia G. Cochrane (Chicago: University of Chicago Press, 2005), 122.

3. Ferry, *Man Made God*, 16.

4. According to Isaiah 43:7, God created us for his glory, and according to John 17:4, glorifying God is what Jesus came to do on the earth.

5. Deuteronomy 6:5 and 1 John 4:8.

6. Mark 12:30-31.

7. Ferry, *What Is the Good Life?*, 255; Luc Ferry, *L'Homme-Dieu ou le sens de la vie* [The Man-God or the meaning of life] (Paris: France Loisirs, 1996), 245.

8. Augustine, *Confessions*, book 1, chapter 1, trans. Albert C. Outler, 1955, https://ccel.org/ccel/augustine/confessions/confessions.iv.html.

9. Ecclesiastes 3:11, NLT.

10. Ernest Renan, *The Future of Science* (Boston: Roberts Brothers, 1891), 89.

11. See Albert Camus, "An Absurd Reasoning," in *The Myth of Sisyphus*, trans. Justin O'Brien (New York: Alfred A. Knopf, 1955), 3.
12. Baron d'Holbach, *The System of Nature: Laws of the Moral and Physical World*, vol. 1, trans. H. D. Robinson (Boston: J. P. Mendum, 1889), 137.
13. André Comte-Sponville, *The Little Book of Atheist Spirituality*, trans. Nancy Huston (New York: Viking, 2006), 51.
14. Blaise Pascal, *The Thoughts of Blaise Pascal*, trans. C. Kegan Paul (London: George Bell and Sons, 1901), 39.

CHAPTER 4: HAPPINESS AT ANY PRICE
1. André Comte-Sponville, *The Little Book of Atheist Spirituality*, trans. Nancy Huston (New York: Viking, 2006), 42.

CHAPTER 5: THE TURNING POINT
1. See, for example, his classic answer in Mark 12:17: "Render to Caesar the things that are Caesar's, and to God the things that are God's." Or his cutting response to a logical dilemma in Mark 12:18-27. Or the way he turns the tables on his adversaries in Mark 11:27-33.
2. John 7:15.
3. Mark 14:60-62.
4. John 14:6.
5. John 14:1.
6. John 14:6.
7. John 3:17.
8. Mark 8:34-35.
9. John 13:1-17.
10. Matthew 20:28.

CHAPTER 6: INTELLECTUAL BARRIERS
1. Ernest Renan, *The Future of Science* (Boston: Robert Brothers, 1892), 40–41.
2. Ferry describes his views of transcendence in *What Is the Good Life?* (University of Chicago Press, 2005).
3. Michel Onfray, *In Defense of Atheism: The Case Against Christianity, Judaism, and Islam*, trans. Jeremy Leggett (Toronto: Viking Canada, 2007), 67.
4. Onfray, *In Defense of Atheism*, 198.
5. Onfray, *In Defense of Atheism*, 101.
6. Genesis 1:28.
7. 1 Corinthians 7:5.
8. Proverbs 5:18-19, NLT.

9. Paul-Henri Thiry d'Holbach, *Christianity Unveiled: Being an Examination of the Principles and Effects of the Christian Religion*, trans. W. M. Johnson (New York: Gordon Press, 1835), 106–107.

10. Baron d'Holbach, *The System of Nature: Laws of the Moral and Physical World*, vol. 1, trans. H. D. Robinson (Boston: J. P. Mendum, 1889), 154.

11. André Comte-Sponville, *The Little Book of Atheist Spirituality*, trans. Nancy Huston (New York: Viking, 2006), 43.

12. Onfray, *In Defense of Atheism*, 105.

13. 1 Corinthians 7:39.

14. Onfray, *In Defense of Atheism*, 83.

15. Onfray, *In Defense of Atheism*, 85.

16. d'Holbach, *Christianity Unveiled*, 98.

17. Renan, *The Future of Science*, 40.

18. d'Holbach, *The System of Nature*, 11.

19. Serge Deruette, *Lire Jean Meslier: curé et athée révolutionnaire* [Reading Jean Meslier: Parish priest and revolutionary atheist] (Brussels: Aden, 2008), 242. Cited quote translated by Lori Varak.

20. Deruette, *Lire Jean Meslier*, 242.

21. Onfray, *In Defense of Atheism*, 83.

22. Onfray, *In Defense of Atheism*, 96.

23. Onfray, *In Defense of Atheism*, 84.

24. Onfray, *In Defense of Atheism*, 84.

25. Michel Onfray, *Traité d'athéologie* [Treatise on atheology] (Paris: Grasset, 2005), 135. Cited quote translated by Lori Varak.

26. Onfray, *In Defense of Atheism*, 95.

27. Jacques Bouveresse, *Peut-on ne pas croire?* [Can we not believe?] (Marseille: Agone, 2007), 217. Cited quote translated by Lori Varak.

CHAPTER 7: SEARCHING FOR CERTAINTY

1. André Comte-Sponville, *The Little Book of Atheist Spirituality*, trans. Nancy Huston (New York: Viking, 2006), 68. Here, Comte-Sponville defines *knowledge* as "the communicable and repeatable result of a demonstration or an experience."

2. Comte-Sponville, *Little Book of Atheist Spirituality*, 71. Italics in the original.

3. Serge Deruette, *Lire Jean Meslier: curé et athée révolutionnaire* [Reading Jean Meslier: Parish priest and revolutionary atheist] (Brussels: Aden, 2008), 121. Cited quote translated by Lori Varak.

4. Deruette, *Lire Jean Meslier*, 113.

5. Jacques Monod, *Chance and Necessity: An Essay on the Natural Philosophy of Modern Biology* (New York: Alfred A. Knopf, 1971), 165.

6. Baron d'Holbach, *The System of Nature: Laws of the Moral and Physical World*, trans. H. D. Robinson (Boston: J. P. Mendum, 1889), 248.
7. Give or take a meter or two; the height varies depending on the snowpack at the summit from year to year.
8. Prosper Alfaric, *Jésus, a-t-il existé?* [Did Jesus exist?] (Paris: Coda, 2005), 50. Cited quote translated by BLF.
9. For a more detailed explanation of this "onomastic" argument, see Richard Bauckham, *Jesus and the Eyewitnesses* (Grand Rapids: Eerdmans, 2017).
10. For example, the Gospels mention the names of tiny local villages such as Bethphage and Chorazin. The Gospel writers knew that Capernaum was situated near water and that sycamore trees grew in Jericho. These arguments come from Peter Williams in his video "New Evidence the Gospels were Based on Eyewitness Accounts," https://www.thegospelcoalition.org/blogs /justin-taylor/new-evidence-that-the-gospels-were-based-on-eyewitness-testimony/.
11. Peter Williams concludes: "Rather than being evidence against the four Gospels, the apocryphal gospels are, in fact, evidence for the four Gospels, because Peter show what would happen if people did make up stories. They are the controlled experiment, if you like, that show what could go on another way," (Excerpt from the lecture "New Evidences the Gospels were Based on Eyewitness Accounts" given by Peter J. Williams at the Lanier Theological Library).
12. Ernest Renan, *The History of the Origins of Christianity, Book 1: Life of Jesus* (London: Mathieson, 1890[?]), 33.
13. Albert Jacquard, *Dieu?* [God?] (Paris: Stock, Bayard, 2003), 86.
14. There is also material from Polybius, dating from roughly 120 years after Alexander, but its reliability is far inferior to that of Arrian.
15. Thanks to Gary Habermas and Mike Licona who suggested I use this argument.
16. Alfaric, *Jésus, a-t-il existé?*, 50.
17. The traditional titles "according to Matthew," "according to Mark," etc., probably appeared in the first half of the second century. No manuscript lists any other authors. The most important historical sources where we find this information are in the writings of Papias of Hieropolis, who is quoted by Eusebius of Caesarea and Irenaeus of Lyon.
18. Alfaric, *Jésus, a-t-il existé?*, 52.
19. For example, the first part of Mark's Gospel; the passion story in Mark's Gospel (which some people claim to be based on another distinct source); another source called Q (from the German *Quelle*, which means "source"), which contains material shared by Matthew and Luke; Matthew's unique material (called M); and Luke's unique material (called L).

20. Deruette, *Lire Jean Meslier*, 122. Cited quote translated by BLF.

21. My discussion of textual criticism was developed in part through personal correspondence with Daniel B. Wallace, executive director of the Center for the Study of New Testament Manuscripts (csntm.org) and senior research professor of New Testament at Dallas Theological Seminary.

CHAPTER 8: MIRACLES: HISTORY OR MYTHOLOGY?

1. Albert Jacquard, *Dieu?* [God?] (Paris: Stock, Bayard, 2003), 109–110. Cited quote translated by Lori Varak.

2. Jacquard, *Dieu?*, 109. Cited quote translated by Lori Varak and the author.

3. Baron d'Holbach, *The System of Nature: Laws of the Moral and Physical World*, vol. 1, trans. H. D. Robinson (Boston: J. P. Mendum, 1889), 35. Italics in the original.

4. Paul Henri Thiry d'Holbach, *Christianity Unveiled: Being an Examination of the Principles and Effects of the Christian Religion*, trans. W. M. Johnson (New York: Gordon Press, 1835), 60.

5. Ernest Renan, *The History of the Origins of Christianity, Book 1: Life of Jesus* (London: Mathieson, [1890?]), 36.

6. Renan, *Origins of Christianity*, 36.

7. Prosper Alfaric, *Jésus a-t-il existé?* [Did Jesus exist?] (Paris: Coda, 2005), 50. Cited quote translated by Lori Varak.

8. Matthew 24; Mark 13; Luke 21.

9. Alfaric, *Jésus a-t-il existé?*, 50.

10. Bertrand Russell, "Why I Am Not a Christian," address to the National Secular Society, London, March 6, 1927. Transcript accessed online at http://schutt.org/files/documents/russell-why_i_am_not_a_christian.pdf, 7.

11. Michel Onfray, *In Defense of Atheism: The Case Against Christianity, Judaism, and Islam*, trans. Jeremy Leggett (Toronto: Viking Canada, 2007), 115.

12. Onfray, *In Defense of Atheism*, 117.

13. Renan, *Origins of Christianity: Life of Jesus*, 41. In the French edition of *Life of Jesus* (*Vie de Jésus*), Renan cites both Suetonius and Tacitus.

14. Onfray, *In Defense of Atheism*, 121.

15. Baron d'Holbach, *Christianity Unveiled*, 28–29.

16. d'Holbach, *Christianity Unveiled*, 7–8.

17. Alfaric, *Jésus a-t-il existé?*, 40–41.

18. Charles Guignebert explains Jensen's position in *Le Problème de Jésus* [The problem of Jesus] (Paris: Coda, 2008), 49–52. Cited quote translated by Lori Varak.

19. Guignebert, *Le Problème de Jésus*, 115. These arguments, and others, can be found in Charles Guignebert's scathing review of mythicist theory.

Interestingly, Guignebert is himself a skeptic who believes we know almost nothing of Jesus.

20. Alfaric, *Jésus a-t-il existé?*, 67.
21. Sylvain Maréchal, *La Fable de Christ dévoilée* [The fable of Christ unveiled] (Paris: Coda, 2010), 44–45. Cited quote translated by Lori Varak.
22. Onfray, *In Defense of Atheism*, 125. Italics in the original.
23. John 21:7, 20. See also John 13:23; 19:26; 20:2.
24. Matthew 17:1; Mark 9:2; Luke 9:28.
25. Alfaric, *Jésus a-t-il existé?*, 76.
26. Alfaric, *Jésus a-t-il existé?*, 57–60.
27. Galatians 1:18-19; 2:1-9.
28. Guignebert, *Le Problème de Jésus*, 157.
29. See, for example, Gary R. Habermas, "The Minimal Facts Approach to the Resurrection of Jesus: The Role of Methodology as a Crucial Component in Establishing Historicity," in *Southeastern Theological Review*, 3.1 Summer 2012, 15–26; Gary R. Habermas and Michael R. Licona, *The Case for the Resurrection of Jesus* (Grand Rapids, MI: Kregel, 2004); Michael R. Licona, *The Resurrection of Jesus: A New Historiographical Approach* (Downers Grove, IL: IVP Academic, 2010); William Lane Craig, *The Son Rises: The Historical Evidence for the Resurrection of Jesus* (Chicago: Moody, 1981).
30. Gary Habermas solidly documents this fact. See, for example, Habermas and Licona, *The Case for the Resurrection of Jesus*.
31. Paul Henri Thiry d'Holbach, *Christianity Unveiled: Being an Examination of the Principles and Effects of the Christian Religion*, trans. W. M. Johnson (New York: Gordon Press, 1835), 46–47.
32. Especially in the Epistle to the Romans and in 1 Corinthians (chapter 15, in particular), where we see him use many rigorous syllogisms.
33. Renan, *Origins of Christianity*, 166.
34. Renan, *Origins of Christianity*, 166.
35. See 1 Corinthians 15:5-8.
36. d'Holbach, *Christianity Unveiled*, 51.

CHAPTER 9: WHERE THE HEAD WENT, THE HEART FOLLOWED

1. Proverbs 16:5.
2. 1 Peter 2:24.
3. Romans 3:10, 12, NLT.
4. John 3:16, NLT.
5. Isaiah 64:6, NLT.
6. Matthew 5:48.
7. Mark 10:26.

8. Mark 10:27.
9. John 3:18.
10. Romans 6:23.
11. Ephesians 2:8-9.
12. Romans 5:1.
13. Romans 6:1-2. See further, Romans 6:3-18.
14. James 2:14-18.
15. Ernest Renan, *The Future of Science* (Boston: Roberts Brothers, 1891), 333.
16. Luke 18:10-14.
17. Serge Deruette, *Lire Jean Meslier: curé et athée révolutionnaire* [Reading Jean Meslier: parish priest and revolutionary atheist] (Brussels: Aden, 2008), 116. Cited quote translated by Lori Varak.
18. Voltaire, *The Works of Voltaire: A Contemporary Version*, vol. III, part II, trans. William F. Fleming (New York: The St. Hubert Guild, 1901), 326.
19. Paul Henri Thiry d'Holbach, *Christianity Unveiled: Being an Examination of the Principles and Effects of the Christian Religion*, trans. W. M. Johnson (New York: Gordon Press, 1835), 96.
20. Renan, *The Future of Science*, 44.
21. Ephesians 4:32.

CHAPTER 10: MOVES AND DEBATES
1. Serge Deruette, *Lire Jean Meslier: curé et athée révolutionnaire* [Reading Jean Meslier: parish priest and revolutionary atheist] (Brussels: Aden, 2008), 273. Cited quote translated by Lori Varak.
2. Deruette, *Lire Jean Meslier*, 142.
3. Paul Henri Thiry d'Holbach, *Christianity Unveiled: Being an Examination of the Principles and Effects of the Christian Religion*, trans. W. M. Johnson (New York: Gordon Press, 1835), 35.
4. Revelation 19:20; 20:10, 14, 15.
5. See, for example, Matthew 8:12, 25:30; Luke 13:25-28; Revelation 2:11, 20:14, 21:8.
6. Bertrand Russell, "Why I Am Not a Christian," address to the National Secular Society, London, March 6, 1927. Transcript accessed online at http://schutt.org/files/documents/russell-why_i_am_not_a_christian.pdf, 7.
7. Deruette, *Lire Jean Meslier*, 273.
8. "A Calvinistical divine, of the name of Petit Pierre, not long since preached and published the doctrine that the damned would at some future period be pardoned. The rest of the ministers of his association told him that they wished for no such thing." See Voltaire, *The Works of Voltaire: A Contemporary Version*, vol. V, part II, trans. William F. Fleming (New York: The St. Hubert Guild, 1901), 21.

9. Voltaire, *The Works of Voltaire: A Contemporary Version*, vol. VII, part II, trans. William F. Fleming (New York: The St. Hubert Guild, 1901), 215.
10. Bertrand Russell, *What I Believe*, Routledge Classics edition (London: Routledge, 2004), 33.
11. Voltaire, *The Works of Voltaire*, vol. VII, part II, 215.
12. Voltaire, *The Works of Voltaire*, vol. VII, part II, 216.
13. Voltaire, *The Works of Voltaire*, vol. VII, part II, 216.
14. Genesis 1:27.
15. Ernest Renan, *The Future of Science* (Boston: Roberts Brothers, 1891), 412.
16. Renan, *The Future of Science*, 412.
17. Richard Dawkins, *The Blind Watchmaker: Why the Evidence of Evolution Reveals a Universe Without Design* (New York: W. W Norton, 1996), 1. Italics added.
18. Francis Crick, *What Mad Pursuit: A Personal View of Scientific Discovery* (New York: Basic Books, 1988), 138. Italics added.
19. Jacques Monod, *Chance and Necessity: An Essay on the Natural Philosophy of Modern Biology* (New York: Alfred A. Knopf, 1971), 109.
20. Monod, *Chance and Necessity*, 21. Italics in the original.
21. Albert Jacquard, *Dieu?* [God?] (Paris: Stock, Bayard, 2003), 12. Cited quote translated by Lori Varak.
22. Monod, *Chance and Necessity*, 143. Italics in the original.
23. I heard this example of the whale from David Berlinski, in the documentary *The Incorrigible Dr. Berlinski*, ColdWater Media, August 2008. An excerpt from this documentary may be found on YouTube, https://www.youtube .com/watch?v=3nxzpHz153Q. Berlinski's comments about turning a cow into a whale run from 0:55 to 4:31.

CHAPTER 11: DISCOVERING APOLOGETICS
1. The word *kalam* refers to the Islamic scholastic theology. It is used in this context because the argument stems mainly from writings from this school of thought, although it also has Christian roots dating back even further.
2. See Genesis 1 and John 1.
3. Bertrand Russell, "Why I Am Not a Christian," address to the National Secular Society, London, March 6, 1927. Transcript accessed online at http://schutt.org/files/documents/russell-why_i_am_not_a_christian.pdf, 7.
4. Voltaire, *The Works of Voltaire: A Contemporary Version*, vol. VI, part I, trans. William F. Fleming (New York: The St. Hubert Guild, 1901), 243–244.
5. Baron d'Holbach, *The System of Nature: Laws of the Moral and Physical World*, vol. 1, trans. H. D. Robinson (Boston: J. P. Mendum, 1889), 22.
6. d'Holbach, *The System of Nature*, 236.

7. Prosper Alfaric, *Jésus, a-t-il existé?* [Did Jesus exist?], 323. Cited quote translated by Lori Varak.
8. Michel Onfray, *In Defense of Atheism: The Case Against Christianity, Judaism, and Islam*, trans. Jeremy Leggett (Toronto: Viking Canada, 2007), 90. Ellipses in the original.
9. "The Big Bang," NASA, July 3, 2007, https://svs.gsfc.nasa.gov/10128.
10. Albert Jacquard, *Dieu?* [God?] (Paris: Stock, Bayard, 2003), 74. Cited quote translated by Lori Varak.
11. Russell, "Why I Am Not a Christian," 2–3.
12. Alfaric, *Jésus, a-t-il existé?*, 323. Cited quote translated by Lori Varak.
13. Serge Deruette, *Lire Jean Meslier: curé et athée révolutionnaire* [Reading Jean Meslier: parish priest and revolutionary atheist] (Brussels: Aden, 2008), 246. Cited quote translated by Lori Varak.
14. André Comte-Sponville, *The Little Book of Atheist Spirituality*, trans. Nancy Huston (New York: Viking, 2006), 87.
15. Comte-Sponville, *The Little Book of Atheist Spirituality*, 88–89. Italics in the original.
16. London School of Theology, in partnership with the University of Middlesex.

EPILOGUE: MY MOTIVATION FOR WRITING

1. Baron d'Holbach, *The System of Nature: Laws of the Moral and Physical World*, vol. 2, trans. H. D. Robinson (Boston: J. P. Mendum, 1889), 325.
2. Ernest Renan, *The Future of Science* (Boston: Roberts Brothers, 1891), 95.
3. James 2:19, italics added.
4. Luke 15:3-7.
5. Luke 15:8-10.
6. Luke 15:11-32.
7. Matthew 13:45-46.
8. Matthew 13:44.
9. Luke 7:36-50. I've adapted the telling of the story slightly for flow. The words in quotation marks throughout are from the biblical text.